Gerhard Kapitzke

# *The Bit and the Reins*

Gerhard Kapitzke

# The Bit and the Reins

## Developing Good Contact and Sensitive Hands

Translated by
Friederike Butler

Trafalgar Square Publishing
North Pomfret, Vermont

First published in 2004 by
Trafalgar Square Publishing
North Pomfret, Vermont 05053
Reprinted 2005
**Printed in Hong Kong**

Title of the original German edition:
*Zügelführung mit Gefühl*
© 2001 BLV Verlagsgesellschaft mbH, München, Germany
English translation © 2004 Trafalgar Square Publishing

ISBN: 1-57076-275-9
Library of Congress Control Number: 2004101556


Illustration credits:
All photos and drawings by the author, except: B. Eylers, pages 9, 94, 125, 129 (bottom); M. Schreiner, page 96.

---

# *Acknowledgments*

I heartily thank the following riders for their mounted help in demonstrating various aspects of holding the reins and rein contract: Jean-Marie Donard, Ruth Giffels, Petra Gnade, Ellen Graepel, Richard Hinrichs, Philippe Karl, Peter Kreinberg, Susanne Neumann, Marlene Rüdebusch; Martina Schlag, Andrea Schmitz, Jutta Szentmiklossy von Primocz, Dr. Iris Vetter, and Claudia Witting. I also wish to thank Bernd Eylers who photographed the pictures on pages 9, 94, 125, and 129 and kindly allowed them to be used here.

# Contents

# Traditions of
## Horsemanship

Undeniably, in the course of history, the horse has proven himself an indispensable servant to mankind. But does man really deserve the horse? Tempers and whips, and even more so, unnatural pressure from bits and reins have tested the horse's patience for thousands of years. Generations of riders believed they had to master the horse both physically and psychologically in order to make him obedient under saddle. However, equestrian experience, as well as common sense, now encourages a two-way partnership based on communication and negotiation rather than the complete submission of one partner to the other.

Horsemanship *means to respect the nature and dignity of our fellow being: the horse. Horsemanship also means to form a trusting relationship between man and horse, without sentimental pampering.*

To this day, reins and bridles are employed as tools of coercion, sometimes due to lack of knowledge but oftentimes despite it. "Riding" does not imply a battle of rider against horse. Riding a horse should be a beautiful dialogue between two friends, and in order to prevent injury, it must be the horse's ability and aptitude that determine the (unfortunately, often exaggerated) expectations of the rider. The rider must always protect the welfare of the animal, far beyond legal requirements, in order to respect the horse as a sensitive fellow being that requires man's help.

Horsemanship expresses itself through respect toward a patient animal that submits to man's will, cannot determine his own life course, and depends on man's mercy. It is also evident when man endeavors to honor the horse's being and nature and meet his needs through fair treatment and gentle riding practices. Horsemanship is not irrevocably bound to one specific style of riding: it can find expression in dressage or on a trail ride. Neither choice of riding style nor a rider's expectations are important; what matters is the physical and psychological harmony between both partners.

Many riders, within the boundaries of their ability, decide to enjoy riding for its own sake and strive to attain complete harmony with their horses. Others see the fulfillment of their passion in competition, and their horses become a means to an end. These riders measure their worth in comparison to others, and the demands they make are directed by competition requirements. Respect for the dignity of a fellow being and in order to prevent costly mistakes, riders must set fair goals in the education of their horses.

Riding is a living, ongoing process for both partners, and it is under the direction of a rider, who is himself not free of failure and mistakes.

Finally, the rider must gain the insight that it is the journey, and the journey alone, that is the goal. A rider who understands this will develop into a person with whom the horse will work in unison. In this sense, rein contact resulting from an independent and balanced seat is essential to developing trust and agreement between horse and rider, and a practical concern for the welfare of the animal is manifested in gentle and empathetic communication through the reins. A horse is a sensitive, living being—not an inanimate, mechanical object that reacts to the pressing of a button. It takes time for a horse and rider to develop as a team, just as it takes time for two people to do the same.

May these few, introductory ideas stimulate sympathetic, empathetic, and judicious riders to continue to honor the ideals of classical horsemanship: The horse should be treated fairly and injury to his health should be avoided—in spite of, and contrary to the modern and commercially falsified equestrian fads of our time. May these ideas also inspire today's young riders to seriously ponder what is written in these pages. To ride well, one must consider the welfare of the horse.

*Horsemanship includes developing the horse gymnastically so it is easier for him to carry a rider's weight. Here, excellent engagement of the hindquarters and a relaxed head and neck carriage are shown in the piaffe.*

# The Nature of the Gaits and Balance

Horses that live amongst their own kind in the wild move with naturally pure gaits. For these horses, the walk is the gait for leisurely feeding. The trot, on the other hand, is the preferred gait when the seasons affect food availability, and they cover longer distances as they change grazing areas. This gait varies from a lazy tempo, to a ground-covering lengthened stride, to the powerful imposing trot of a stallion. The horse's third gait ranges from a pleasant three-beat canter—an expression of a love of life and exuberant play, complete with flying changes in turns—to a lurching four-beat gallop over rough, rock-covered ground, to a stretched-out race to escape supposed danger.

Young stallions, in their play fighting rituals, conduct maneuvers that can be considered the natural basis for dressage exercises. In all the various movements, the horse's head and neck extend above his body—the main support of the limbs—serving as a swinging pendulum weight and counterbalance and preventing staggering or falling. The repertoire of a horse's natural movements can indicate his strengths and limitations in the realm of dressage training.

The serious dressage trainer *always* keeps in mind the purity of the gaits, and his demands never exceed the natural ability of the horse. And, in fact, a rider must train and strengthen the natural gaits so that his horse is able to carry his weight without stress. These criteria should be at the heart of any dressage training program.

*Joyful leaps of the stabled horse when turned out clearly show the horse's need to stretch his neck and back musculature.*

At the start of training, the rider must move with the young horse's rhythm as his mount learns to find his balance under the extra weight. The rider must not disturb or interfere with the horse; he may give supportive—but not demanding—aids. This is particularly true in the case of rein aids; they must never be forceful and interfere with a horse's search for balance. A rider who has observed and, therefore, has a mental image of how horses move in the wild, will strive to transfer this image into his training and avoid creating unnatural movement through forceful aids. It is of the utmost importance not to change the horse's natural way of going, but instead to foster balance and strengthen a horse's carrying and locomotive power through gymnastic training.

When stabled horses are turned out in a large paddock and allowed to move freely, they will express themselves through motion. The stallion will pull out all the stops and give it all he has: he will "strut his stuff" with floating trot steps; he will gallop madly—often bucking simultaneously; and he will perform wild caprioles. His raised head, lightly flexed poll, and imposingly curved neck will make him appear larger than he is. Commandingly, he will throw his head up and stare intensely at the horizon, his nostrils flared as he scents the air. His boastful appearance is meant to intimidate his rivals as much as it is meant to impress receptive mares, or perhaps, it is merely meant to express his great delight at having escaped the limitations of his stall. After being confined, stallions will happily lower their heads and stretch their backs while trotting. Mares, on the other hand, tend to convey their pleasure in more measured ways.

When running free in any gait, as well as in turns and jumps, the horse will use his head and neck as a balancing rod to maintain his equilibrium and avoid falling. Though head position will vary greatly, the neck will be stretched out as an effective compensatory balance for the rest of the body, similar to the tail of a cat or squirrel, which functions as a steering tool when either animal is climbing or jumping. Observing the horse's natural movement should teach the rider not to disturb his partner's need for balance under saddle, but rather to support the horse's center of gravity through empathetic aids, making his own weight as tolerable as possible. In practice, this means that the rider must master rein aids independent of his seat,

allow the horse to stretch forward and downward after every strenuous exercise, and flex the poll only to the point where the horse's face is still in front of the vertical and his neck is not too short. In this manner, horse and rider can find their way to balance together.

The German language abounds in bridling and "bitting" idiom, implying discipline or holding something in check. Corresponding English idiom might be: "keeping a tight rein" on a situation, "curbing" someone's appetite, "bridling" in a show of anger, or "chomping at the bit." These expressions derive from the equestrian world. Many riders hang onto these idiomatic meanings and mistake reins and bridles as

*The posture of a horse running free shows symmetrical balance and natural, "on the bit" head carriage. At the beginning of the young horse's education, the rider works with the natural rhythm and movement of the horse and avoids interfering with disruptive aids. The posture of both these horses is the same; the rider's rein contact does not hinder the horse's natural head and neck carriage.*

*This is an example of a horse running free and using his head and neck as a balancing device. The body of the horse is leaning toward the right into the turn, while his upright head and neck, functioning like a "balancing rod," swings to the left, counter-balancing and stabilizing the tilt to the right.*

instruments of force. Rein aids that painfully seesaw a horse's head behind the vertical border on animal torture and are completely devoid of any sense of horsemanship. They counteract any forward aids, and in fact, result in backward riding, "braking" the forward momentum, as well as disturbing, and often making impossible, the horse's search for balance.

By keeping in mind the horse's natural balancing behavior, the rider realizes that he must interfere as little as possible with the horse's head and neck carriage. The horse has to learn to incorporate the saddle and rider's weight in his search for balance. The

rider will disturb this process if he sits incorrectly in the saddle and forces the "balancing rod" of the horse behind the vertical.

A good example of this is the piaffe. Here, the horse loses some of his stability because the area over which he stands is reduced, and he stands alternately on only two legs. The effects of the rein aids become particularly clear here. Empathetic, soft rein contact allows for harmonious rider-horse equilibrium, whereas forced rein manipulation can throw the horse completely off balance.

Because the rider especially uses and

*The need of the free-moving horse to stretch his neck and back musculature strongly indicates to the rider that he must allow, not only the young horse, but also the more advanced horse, to stretch frequently, particularly after every strenuous dressage exercise.*

stresses the horse's mouth and back, he must protect them from being damaged. The horse suffers quietly, so it is the rider's duty to recognize problems in time and resolve them. He must be aware that any bridle of any construction is as soft or hard on the horse's mouth as the hand that controls it. Some bridle and bit constructions, in rough hands, will increase pain, and consequent damage to a horse manifold. This is why a basic knowledge of bridling and bitting is absolutely mandatory for every rider.

An individually and correctly fitted bridle that prevents pressure and pain is a prerequisite for harmonious contact. There is an old saying that warns you not to "look a gift horse in the mouth." However, whether a gift or not, it is crucial that every rider

conscientiously look into his horse's mouth in order to determine its anatomical makeup. Then, he must try to find and test the most appropriate bit until the horse shows himself to be satisfied. A horse that is in constant pain due to an ill-fitting or damaging bit cannot possibly go in a relaxed manner under the rider. He will be forever distracted, will not respond to sensitive aids, and will become withdrawn and impervious to rider influence.

The reins and the bridle form the silent medium of communication between the rider's hands and the horse's mouth. Through the reins and the bridle, the rider negotiates with the horse regarding direction, balanced movement, and more importantly, the gymnasticizing of the horse's body that will enable it to round itself under the rider's weight like an elastic steel spring into bow-like collection. The rein contact gathers the forward energy of the horse, regulating the driving aids of the legs and seat that always precede the rein aids. The synchronized and harmonious aids of the dressage rider not only aid the horse's ability to carry him, they also allow the horse to move as freely as possible without forceful interference.

By nature, the horse's back was not intended to carry the weight of a rider, despite the fact that positioning a saddle on the horse's back seems to invite the rider to mount and seems "made for" the rider's seat. This appearance deceives: the muscling of the back is primarily constructed to carry the spine. When the horse's back is burdened with the rider's weight, the back muscles and the spine actually bend downward a bit. The tips of the dorsal spinous processes touch and grate against one another, the connecting ligaments of the spine are strained, and the cartilage discs between the vertebrae are pressed together at the top and separated at the bottom. The consequence is that the even buffer function of the cartilage discs is impeded. In the long run, the rider's weight may lead to pain, tightening and hardening of the back muscles, and inelastic calcification of the spine. The back of the horse may become hard, like a board, as he develops into a "leg mover" with a back that no longer

**Collection in the Piaffe, the So-Called "Trot on the Spot"** The horse rounds himself into an elastic and spring-like bow; the hindquarters lower themselves, and the hind legs step further and further under the croup, lightening the forehand and taking on a portion of the rider's weight. The lifting of the head and neck must not be disturbed.

swings and a trot that bounces the rider out of the saddle with every step.

This is the reason for strengthening the musculature of the back through gymnastic exercise and massage so that it can carry the additional weight of the rider elastically and with spring, without pushing the spine downward and causing pain. Exercises for longitudinal bending and the gymnasticizing of the haunches—in hand and under saddle—allow the back muscles to round upward. These, as well as daily massages of the saddle area, will strengthen the back muscles so that they can carry weight and lift the spine. The horse will develop into a desirable "back mover," allowing the rider to swing along in an elastic and relaxed manner.

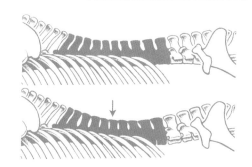

The Spine's Burden

*Above:* The spine of the horse in its natural position, without the weight of a rider. The dorsal spinal processes of the spine maintain their appropriate distance. The area where the saddle sits (approximately the eleventh thoracic vertebra to the second lumbar vertebra) is shaded.

Below: The spine is bent downward by the weight of the rider (indicated by the arrow). Weak back musculature may allow the dorsal spinous processes to touch, straining the connecting ligaments between the vertebrae and causing painful inflammation that will lead to eventual calcification.

*If you want to become an expert, start developing an independent seat at an early age.*

# An Independent Seat and Rein Contact

The basis of all riding, and every riding style, is a balanced seat that is, in all circumstances, in harmony with the horse's center of gravity and complemented by the rider's independent and sensitive rein contact.

The initial driving aids of the rider's seat, weight, and thighs determine the forward movement of the horse. Only then is there a place for rein aids that may correct, support, complement, or underline what has been asked, regulating the forward pushing power of the horse. Without the preceding driving effect, the restraining and limiting rein aids lose their purpose—even in the transition from a half-halt to the halt. Any swaying or movement of the rider should not be involuntarily transferred to his hands, and therefore, to the horse's mouth.

A prerequisite for mastering precise rein aids is the rider's education on the longe line, where he can practice a balanced seat without "holding on." A rider who has not learned an independent seat with independent rein contact will grab onto the reins in moments

of insecurity and will, without necessarily intending to do so, pull on the horse's mouth. Only a seat that is well-balanced in any situation will allow a rider to use very refined rein aids, free from any pulling or yanking.

Beginner riders, who slide in the saddle and lose their balance, are subconsciously tempted to hold onto the reins. The horse does not understand the involuntary, accidental pressure or the continuous pulling on his mouth. Because there are no preceding driving aids, he feels himself unjustly punished. A horse that suffers from mouth pain due to a rider's hard hands, or perhaps due to an incorrectly fitted or defective bit, will either try to withdraw from the rein aids or fight them. Not only will his head and neck become tense, but also his back musculature, and the rider will no longer be able to swing in harmony with the horse. Consequently, the rider's weight and leg aids will become inexact, and the horse will reject them.

The education of a beginner rider should start on a trained and relaxed schoolmaster that will excuse and forgive incorrect aids without negative consequences for the rider.

Above: *The stallion at liberty displays the natural "rough draft" of the passage.*
Below: *A "rein independent" seat. The reins are looped; the horse maintains collection and self-carriage in the passage and is not forced into an unnatural frame.*

## Comparing a "Rein Independent" Seat and a "Rein Dependent" Seat

*Left:* The outward appearance of the "rein independent" seat in the passage. The looped reins indicate that the rider is not "holding on" with the reins; he is sitting upright, centered and balanced in the saddle, supported only by the stirrups. The rein contact comes from loose, flexible hands that do not transfer any body movement to, or inadvertently pull on, the horse's mouth. A bend in the elbows allows for a little "give" forward of the hands, as for example, for letting the horse stretch forward and downward. The rider sits deep "into the horse"; the seat and thigh aids are continually effective and assume a large part of the aids. The horse's ears are turned attentively back toward the rider; his neck is not too short, and his face remains in front of the vertical. The horse is cooperating completely with the rein aids.

*Right:* An incorrect, "rein dependent" seat. The rider hangs on to taut reins, pulls the horse's head behind the vertical, and shortens his neck. The rider's upper body leans too far back; his seat bones push forward and hard into the saddle, burdening the forehand; and his straight arms transfer every jerk to the horse's mouth. The effect of the seat is lost as the rider allows himself to be pulled along, and pressure from his seat and force from the reins counteract one another. The rider does not sit balanced at the center of gravity, and his toes point outward, his spurs digging into the horse's flanks. The horse attempts to escape the rider's force by running forward. Demonstrations of this "yank and spur" style can often be observed at horse shows, particularly in the extended trot.

The horse should be longed on a circle with side-reins that stabilize his head and neck carriage, and the student should ride without stirrups or reins. At first, he can hold onto a "bucking strap" at the front of the saddle. It is less advisable to allow the student to hold onto the front of the saddle itself (and thus "pull his seat into the saddle") as it eliminates some room for movement in the search for balance and a certain necessary "looseness" of the seat. The rider's whole posture can become cramped and tight. As the rider becomes more secure, he will balance himself in the saddle and lean inward, according to the circle's centrifugal force. Eventually, he will be able to swing his arms and twist his waist in exercises while remembering that his seat must remain solid and still in the saddle.

His knees should lie flat on the saddle flap without clamping, and his lower legs should hang down loosely. The tempo can increase slowly from walk, to trot, to canter, and eventually, the beginner rider can take up the reins and the stirrups. This can be difficult for a new rider because he must remember not to hang on the reins and be careful not to lose the stirrups.

After some time, when the rider has mastered holding loose reins without real contact and can softly maintain his stirrups without standing in them, then the rider—on his schoolmaster, and perhaps still with side-reins—moves off the longe line and onto the track of the whole arena, in order to practice giving the aids and establishing rein contact. Thus, the rider's balanced and centered seat

*The beginner learns on the longe line to sit balanced in the saddle without using her hands or reins. This way, she is not tempted to hold onto the reins for security. When she feels unstable, she holds onto the front of the saddle, or preferably, a "bucking strap." (The longe line is always attached to a longeing cavesson and never to the bit.) Once her seat is balanced, the rider may take up the reins and stirrups, in order to practice rein contact and elastic use of the stirrups (keeping her heels down).*

on the longe line is a prerequisite for developing independent rein contact that transmits precise rein aids and prevents pain in the horse's mouth.

Communication between the rider's hand and the horse's mouth must be completely without force, somewhat like a conversation between friends. The friendship does not preclude that, at times, it is necessary to give a short, energetic, and decisive reminder of admonishment at the exact moment a horse is resistant. This reminder will stay in the horse's memory. Admonishing rein aids, therefore, should never be cruel, or brutal, or result in permanent pulling or yanking.

The "punishing" rein aid can express itself, for example, as a consequence of the driving aids by briefly bending the horse's head behind the vertical, confining and shortening his neck, and causing the horse temporary discomfort.  The subsequent "giving" of the reins is a reward, as well as a

*Children often learn from the beginning to sit in the saddle without tension or fear of losing their balance, and they seem to learn an independent seat almost as if they are playing a progressive game: first on the longe line, then in hand, and finally, on their own, away from either the longe or lead line.*

moment of relaxation for the horse. Skillful rein aids are characterized more by yielding or softening, than by taking or restricting. The varying rein pressure on the more advanced horse's mouth primarily consists of a kind of light "plucking" on a corner of the mouth and tongue, usually on one side, in order to alert the horse and introduce a new exercise.

Rein contact is a live connection between the rider's hands and the horse's mouth; it is an energetic game of question and answer that does not tolerate disruption. The horse will not understand a vague taking or giving of the reins that is not related to the seat and leg aids. In order to maintain rein contact with the horse's mouth, the rider's hands must follow the horse's head movement—even if

it is, at times, an evasive movement. The rein contact must not become tight or backward. The principle of using short, repeated half-halts, if necessary, is based on the theory of reprimand and praise. "Taking" the reins is an admonishment and rebuke, while "giving" allows relaxation and so is a reward.

The traditional expressions of "half" and "full" halts (in German, *halbe* and *ganze Parade*) often lead to misunderstanding and, therefore, should be struck from equestrian vocabulary. A half-halt, in its basic form, consists of momentary tension on the reins, which transmits to the mouth—more or less, an intensive "plucking" that, with an advanced horse, acts more on the tongue and corners of the mouth than on the bars (the

*Half-halts can be used for admonishment or rebuke for inattentiveness or resistance. The horse's profile goes briefly behind the vertical, then the subsequent giving of the reins relaxes the horse's neck and allows his face to return in front of the vertical in both reward and praise.*

*During the training phase, the hands follow the relaxed movement of the horse's head and maintain a light contact without hindering his movement. The horse gains the impression that contact in any head-and-neck position will be maintained, without restriction or confinement. The rider's deep seat "into the horse" remains stationary. In contrast to the stretching exercise in the beginning stages of training, here, the rider allows stretching, but only with rein contact and without relieving the horse's back of her weight.*

gap between the front incisor teeth and back molars on the lower jaw where the bit rests). The pressure of this rein aid on the mouth can vary, depending on what is necessary, from a light, energetic jolt to a very slight indication on one or both reins. If, for example, the horse does not react, or reacts slowly to a half-halt preparing for a full halt, then the rein aid must be repeated several times in quick succession, until the horse is standing still. Early in training, the horse may react gradually, but as training progresses and his haunches are lowered, the horse must begin to react much more quickly. Upon completion of training, when the haunches are powerfully muscled, the slightest indication of tension on the reins should bring the horse—on his own accord—instinctively to a halt. Every half-halt is preceded by driving seat and thigh aids to encourage the hind legs to step under and the hindquarters to assume more weight and maintain the forward pushing power that is regulated by the rein aids.

*A Western riding demonstration of a "rein independent" seat, without a bridle or reins. The horse reacts reflex-like to the seat and thigh aids, performing a turn on the haunches.*

## Collection in Balance

Dressage is based on the principal of *collection in balance*. Rein aids maintain the constant connection between the rider's hands and the horse's mouth; they regulate the amount of forward movement, and they stabilize the gaits. The horse rounds himself—the most extreme example of this being the piaffe—within the frame of driving seat and thigh aids and receiving rein aids. He is like a curved, taut bow or an elastic and compressed steel spring. His croup is lowered, his head and neck raised, and his profile remains just in front of the vertical. His hind end comes under his body and carries more weight. The rider's hands communicate with the horse's mouth in a constant variation of give-and-take, without exerting any kind of forceful pressure. Thus, the horse's neck curves upward naturally, unrestricted. With powerful locomotion from behind, the horse

marches with impulsion, cadence, and balance: in essence, the horse "carries himself."

The purpose of gymnasticizing is to strengthen the horse's back so he will be able to carry a rider's weight over time without injury. There are three phases of development that lead to collection. Depending on the aptitude of the horse, these may take six to eight years to complete. The first phase focuses on stretching—that is, the maximum stretching of the horse's body—in each gait, so that the musculature of the back is tightened and stretched, and the horse can rediscover his equilibrium under the rider and balance himself. For gymnasticizing and strengthening, the stretching position must be asked for—and allowed—again and again, even after training is completed, and on into old age. During this exercise, the rider should lighten his seat to unburden the horse's back.

The second phase is based on the

*Important Stages of Training Under the Rider*
*Above: At first, the horse searches for a deep*
*balance by lowering his head and neck. The*
*horse's body is allowed to fully stretch, the*
*reins are given completely, the horse's back is*
*not burdened, the back musculature is*
*stretched, and the hind legs step unhampered*
*and energetically forward.*
*Middle: The beginning of dressage-like*
*training. Here, the horse learns to carry the*
*rider's weight in balance and step*
*rhythmically.*
*Below: Collection in the passage. The*
*horse's profile remains in front of the*
*vertical, his head and neck are unrestricted*
*and so can serve as a "balancing rod" for*
*combined equilibrium.*
*During the whole training process, two*
*essential characteristics stand out: The*
*hindquarters become more engaged and step*
*increasingly further under the horse's body,*
*lowering the croup, which, in turn, leads to*
*the raising of the neck and head as a counter*
*balance.*

working posture—that is, the horse's natural carriage. The rider gradually, and carefully molds this posture by encouraging the hind legs to step under energetically, longitudinally flexing the horse's raised head at the poll, stabilizing their joint equilibrium, and controlling and promoting the impulsion and rhythm of the gaits.

Finally, the third phase leads to the culmination of collection: the hind legs step under the body the furthest, the hocks bend the most, and the haunches carry the maximum weight. The horse's top line is rounded like a taut, but elastic bow, permitting the rider to swing along in harmony.

In the piaffe, the dual limb support becomes smaller, and the horse's balance

Above: *A stallion at liberty, meaning to impress bystanders with his trot, and the same stallion shown in collected passage. The riderless, uncollected horse develops forward impulsion from his outstretched hindquarters in a free, upright position. He appears altogether stretched and relaxed, his body remaining in a horizontal position.*

Below: *On the other hand, the mounted, collected horse appears shorter, more compact, and rounder; his body aims slightly forward and upward. His hind legs step increasingly further under his body, his croup is lowered, and as a result, his head and neck lift. The forward energy aims upward and transforms into carrying power; the horse resembles an elastic steel spring that rocks the rider's weight on a rounded back. The soft and giving rein contact in the photograph is admirable.*

*In the piaffe, support for the limbs is insecure because the support base alters with the stepping of the diagonal pairs of feet. These diagonal feet are closer together than they are normally. Altogether, the support base is reduced to about half of its normal size, and the horse's balance is much more unstable. Here, again, commendable soft and giving rein contact is displayed.*

under the rider becomes unstable. (At the same time, the horse is more easily controlled by the rider.) The horse's insecure stance requires that the rider sit completely balanced at the center of gravity in the saddle, and he must support the horse in his search for stability through light, rhythmical rein contact that does not interfere with the balancing function of the head and neck. Despite a longitudinal flexing at the poll, the horse's neck must not be shortened—it must retain its naturally upright, long, and relaxed carriage.

In collection, the desired rounding of the back muscles is attained by increasing the engagement of the hindquarters under the horse's body and varying the bend of the hocks, which is seen most distinctly in the piaffe. When the rein contact is very short and tight with strong flexion at the poll—forcing the horse's neck to "roll in" and his face behind the vertical—the whole neck and back musculature tightens up and locks in extreme tension, bouncing the rider hard in the saddle. In addition, because of this shortening of the neck, the horse is prevented from finding his balance under the rider's weight. Step sequences lose their impulsion, and the steps themselves become shorter, stomping, and insecure. On the other hand, if the horse is allowed to carry his head in a free and upright position in front of the vertical, then his back muscles swing with variable elasticity in the step sequence, and the rider bounces only minimally, swinging

In the piaffe, correct, yielding rein contact (*Above*) compared to incorrect, forceful rein contact (*Below*). The incorrectly handled reins pull the head and neck down with a seesaw motion, the neck shows an incorrect break, and the neck and back musculature is overstressed. The horse cannot balance the rider's additional weight, so his trot steps are short and unstable.

along softly in the rhythm of the steps. With his free "balancing rod," the horse is able to find his center of gravity without a problem, and he can step with impulsion and energy without losing his balance.

## The Conversation between the Rider's Hands and the Horse's Mouth

- *If a rider insists on overpowering and dominating his mount, he will not develop a relaxed and tranquil harmony with his horse.*

- *If a rider always strives to raise, shorten, or confine his horse's head and neck with the reins, then he misunderstands the fundamental principle that rein aids are always secondary and used to accompany other aids.*

- *Reins must not be thought of as solid and unyielding "railroad ties" that need to be manipulated by brute strength; rather, they ought to be considered thin, flexible poles with enough "give" to allow the horse's neck a certain amount of freedom.*

- *Soft rein contact invites the horse to stretch with a long neck into the bit in a relaxed manner, accept the rein aids willingly and freely, and answer these aids with peaceful chewing.*

- *The horse's head and neck must be free to act as a "balancing rod," as the horse finds and supports a shared equilibrium under the rider's weight.*

- *Successful empathetic rein contact is characterized by a continuous, soft dialogue between the rider's hands and the horse's tongue and largely foregoes exerting pressure on the lower jaw.*

# Protecting the
## Horse's Mouth

Basically, a rider must differentiate between bridles that employ a bit (a snaffle or curb, for example) and those that do not affect the horse's mouth but primarily put pressure on the bridge of the nose. An example is the *longeing cavesson*, a valuable and effective aid for training and educating both the horse and rider. In the case of the cavesson, half-halts are relayed through brief pressure on the bridge of the nose that varies in severity, and which the horse reacts to through nerve reflexes. Consistent, unrelenting pressure would only bring about counter-pressure and an uncontrollable horse. For the rider, the cavesson works best when it is used with two reins in conjunction with a snaffle bridle. It teaches the young horse about bending at the poll, turning, and halting in a gentle manner, and without exerting pressure on his mouth.

For trail riding, particularly in high traffic areas, the cavesson is not recommended unless accompanied by additional bridling and a bit, as in situations of fright or panic, the rider may be unable to stop his horse. Also, collecting the horse under the rider is not possible with just a cavesson because the horse's chewing activity is limited and individualized rein contact cannot be achieved.

The basic and most crucial element of the longeing cavesson is the nosepiece made of iron. It is fitted as closely as possible to the curves of the bridge of the nose and stitched onto smooth leather. It rests over the horse's nasal bone. The better the fit, the less chance

*Leading a young horse with a cavesson ensures obedience.*

there is that the nosepiece will be pulled sideways when the horse is longed. The headpiece (the combination of the crown and cheekpieces) keeps the nosepiece at the desired height on the horse's nose. The cheekpieces are attached to the nosepiece, and both are connected, if necessary, with additional straps so that the heavy iron nosepiece remains in a horizontal position and does not tilt downward. A jowl strap is attached to the cheekpieces to prevent them from slipping into the horse's eyes when the longe line is pulled from the side. The browband and throatlatch are superfluous.

## The Cavesson and its Varying Functions

- *Prior to the start of actual training, the cavesson serves as a halter for leading the young horse.*

- *The cavesson protects the horse's sensitive mouth while he is longed and worked in hand.*

- *The cavesson teaches a young horse the beginning rein aids, without inflicting mouth pain.*

- *When a rider uses the cavesson in combination with a snaffle bit, he can transition the rein aids from the cavesson to the bit in a gradual manner, maintaining the sensitivity of the horse's mouth from the start.*

- *When using the cavesson instead of a normal bridle, a beginner rider's faulty rein aids are directed toward the horse's less sensitive nasal bone rather than his mouth.*

- *The cavesson is invaluable for horses with tooth problems or mouth wounds that temporarily cannot tolerate a bit.*

*Beginning a dressage education
with the cavesson and snaffle.*

The chin strap holds the iron nosepiece in position. The nosepiece must not be padded in order to allow the horse to feel the effect of the pressure. On the other hand, the crown, jowl, and chin straps should be lightly padded in order to ensure a fairly snug fit and to prevent chafing. The chewing activity of the horse must not be impaired, however. The nosepiece is bent outward on each side so the horse's cheeks are not rubbed raw. Attached to the nosepiece are three D-rings for lead or longe lines and riding reins. The two outside rings have long "stems" in order to emphasize the rider's rein aids.

This fairly basic, light cavesson model corresponds to the centuries-proven Spanish cavesson, though it is far less severe. (The Spanish model has metal "teeth" called *Serreta* lining the inner edge of the nosepiece.) Instead, the pressure on the bridge of the nose is caused by the weight of the nosepiece itself, which is intensified by the tightening of either rein.

There are a number of different types of cavessons available from equine suppliers that have additional—and unnecessary—leather straps and buckles, as well as thick padding, but these do not serve the purpose of training the horse. The half-halts cannot be relayed, and in an emergency situation, you could not control a disobedient horse with such a cavesson. These types of cavessons are based on an erroneous sense of kindness toward animals and a misunderstanding of the nature of the horse. The simple cavesson described previously is an optimal tool for training the horse obedience and familiarizing him with longeing and the beginnings of rider rein contact while inflicting little pain and protecting his mouth.

When using the cavesson while leading the horse, longeing, and doing exercises in hand, the trainer must carefully imitate the horse's body language and behavior in order to be clearly understood. A quiet voice command should always precede a half-halt. The horse should comprehend that every command that is not obeyed is followed by a painful jerk on the bridge of his nose. Soon,

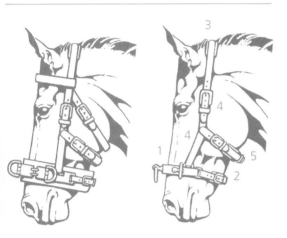

## Cavesson Variations ▲

*Left:* A wide and thickly padded nosepiece. Half-halts will not be communicated through the padding to the bridge of the nose, and the throatlatch and browband are superfluous. As a training and educational tool, this style of cavesson is worthless.

*Right:* The basic construction of a multi-purpose cavesson, without the unnecessary throatlatch or browband: ① An iron nosepiece with three dee rings sewn onto the leather and without sharp edges (or *Serrata*); ② A padded jawband; ③ A padded crownpiece; ④ Cheekpieces that are attached in a forward position to the nosepiece; ⑤ A jowl strap to hold the cheekpieces away from the eyes.

## Ineffective and Effective Cavessons ▶

*Above:* An ineffective cavesson, overly padded, with too much extraneous leather.
*Below:* A simple, multi-purpose cavesson with three rings, based on the Spanish model.

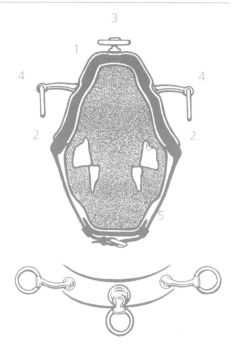

## The Cavesson Nosepiece

A cross section of the horse's head at the height of the front molars.

1. The iron nosepiece must be fitted as closely as possible to the shape of the horse's nose to prevent the cavesson from slipping to the side, for example, when the longe line is being pulled.
2. The outward-bending ends of the nosepiece prevent sideways pressure on the molars and enable chewing activity without chafing.
3. The middle, movable ring on its short stem is used for longeing and exercises in hand.
4. The side rings on their long stems (approximately 2 1/2 inches long) are for reins, double longe lines, and long reining. The rings should be attached to their stems firmly so they do not jingle or clang in a distracting manner.
5. The chin strap with padding between the buckle and chin.
6. The molars.

the horse will react obediently in anticipation of the voice alone, without the actual half-halt. The trainer must not fumble conspicuously or uncontrollably, speak more than necessary, or become loud so that he inadvertently challenges the horse and appears to be an opponent the horse should react to assertively.

The use of the cavesson allows a completely uneducated yearling to be trained obedience in a simple manner. Even after it is no longer utilized, the cavesson's effect remains permanently in the horse's memory. It is almost impossible to hold an impetuous two-year-old when leading him with a normal halter, nor is it easy to reprimand the youngster, if necessary. However, a few strong tugs on the cavesson with the lead line by casually and inconspicuously flexing your

*In cases of unreasonable and extreme opposition from a horse, the cavesson can be temporarily adjusted to fit in a low position over the nose. All horses will respect this harsh consequence.*

*A short, powerful tug—
stemming from the wrist—
induces even the most
misbehaved stallion to accept
the leadership of his trainer.*

wrist, results in an immediate pressure sensation on the horse's nasal bone and is sufficient. Brief and energetic tugs at the moment of disobedience—only then, and employed as sparingly as possible—induce obedience in even the most misbehaved stallions. The effect is lasting, as the horse stores the momentary pain in his memory, and the cavesson soon becomes redundant. If the trainer employs the half-halts as described, the horse will not associate him with the pain, but will have the impression that he has punished himself by misbehaving or disobeying. Power struggles, and fights between man and animal will thus be avoided.

The painful tug to the bridge of the nose, normally employed infrequently and without causing injury, may at first appear rough, but

it does, in fact, correspond to natural horse behavior. Horses are by no means squeamish with one another when it comes to establishing and challenging rank. The horse accepts the effect of the cavesson without defensive behavior because there is no apparent antagonist. Therefore, the cavesson, despite its resounding effect, can be considered horse-friendly because of its brief application and short-lived pain.

In order to protect the young horse's mouth when first longeing him, for a brief period of time, he should be outfitted with only the cavesson. After a while, in addition to the cavesson, the horse can be tacked with a snaffle bridle and either draw or side reins. The longe line can be attached to either the middle or inner ring on the cavesson; that way, the force of the longe is lessened somewhat, and the cavesson will remain in position on the horse's head. Under no circumstances should the longe line be attached to the inner snaffle ring, as the outside snaffle ring will be pulled into the horse's mouth, putting painful pressure on

**Leading in Hand**
In a cavesson, the young horse learns to walk with his trainer at his shoulder. Half-halts on the nasal bone insist on obedience.

In addition to being a great tool for longeing, the cavesson is suitable for loosening and collecting exercises in hand. The lead line should be attached to the inner side ring on the cavesson so that a strong half-halt does not pull the outer cheek piece into the horse's outer eye. If the horse is having problems staying in the right direction, then the lead line should be attached to the middle ring. The trainer should remain in the area of the horse's shoulder, behind the horse's eye, in order to optically exert a driving effect. He should remain upright, quiet, and at arm's distance, though in the horse's range of vision. If the horse pushes toward the trainer, half-halts, vibrations of the lead line, or the trainer's hand moving the horse's head away encourage the horse to remain at a distance. Every exercise should begin with a vocal request given shortly before the application of

the tongue and bars. In response, the horse will cramp his neck musculature.

Side reins should be adjusted so that the horse's neck is not shortened or confined, and his profile should remain in front of the vertical. At the same time, the radius of movement—particularly the lowering and raising—of the head and neck is limited. If the rather rigid side reins are fastened so they are too short, then the horse's tongue and bars may be rubbed sore by the pulling action on the snaffle. Draw reins are usually more suitable as they permit the horse more freedom to adjust and vary his head and neck position, relieving tension as necessary. By using a cavesson, the half-halts affect only the horse's nose, and the horse can move the snaffle into the most comfortable position on his tongue and bars.

**Longeing with a Cavesson and Draw Reins**
The longe line is attached to the cavesson so the horse's mouth is not affected. The draw reins glide smoothly and variably through the rings of the snaffle, and the horse has the freedom to adjust his head position.

*The cavesson is essential for longe work in order to protect the horse's mouth. The longe line must never be hooked to a snaffle ring. The cavesson enables the trainer to exhibit authority and leadership as the "herd boss."*

the aid. The cavesson can be used by itself, at first, followed by the addition of a snaffle bridle and side reins.

The cavesson is of multifaceted benefit both to the education of the horse under the rider and the training of a beginner rider. Combining the snaffle bit with the cavesson almost painlessly familiarizes the horse's sensitive mouth with the bit. The rider controls two sets of reins, and in the beginning, the aids are given solely via the nasal bone, allowing the snaffle to rest passively in the horse's mouth. Once the horse learns to react to the pressure on his nose, the rider can begin a smooth transition to the snaffle aids with light pressure and "play" on the tongue and bars.

The cavesson reins are attached to the two outer rings, and their aids clarify turns and instigate a light, longitudinal bending at the poll, without confining the horse's neck. The snaffle aids, through very refined play of the rein hands, raise the head and neck. The

*Work in hand with the cavesson, lead line, and side reins. The trainer maintains an arm's length distance in order to remain in the horse's range of vision.*

**Training in Hand**

The lead line (an approximately 6 foot long leather shank) is snapped or buckled onto the middle or inner ring of the cavesson. When combined with the cavesson, the lead line serves as an educational device for the horse. A few short, hard tugs to the nose teach the horse obedience while protecting his sensitive mouth. For work in hand, in addition to the cavesson and lead line, the horse is equipped with a simple snaffle bridle and side reins. The lead line (identified by the arrow) is held at the appropriate length with the left hand while the whip is in the right hand—and vice versa. The cavesson's jawband is buckled under the cheekpieces of the bridle so that the snaffle bit remains flexible. Experienced trainers prefer side reins without rubber "donuts" so the head and neck can only stretch to a constant, measured point.

rein aids to the cavesson consist of reflex-like, short, alternating taking and giving—sort of a little nudges, or reminders, to bend at the poll—but are in no way of a lasting or forceful nature. Quite on the contrary, they communicate to the horse that he may relax his neck at any time. Under no circumstances should the horse ever be forced to rigidly bend at the poll with his face behind the vertical.

In the same manner, the cavesson can protect the mouth of the school horse from the clumsy and unpracticed hands of the beginner rider. The rider can primarily using the cavesson reins to practice rein aids and allow the snaffle reins to hang, slightly looped. This also teaches the beginner rider to deal with two sets of reins from the start, which, of course, is valuable for any subsequent dressage education with a double bridle. When both sets of reins are of equal length, then the lowering and lifting of the horse's head will result in an alternating effect of rein pressure on the horse's mouth and

*The tack used early in the horse's education under the rider: a cavesson and a snaffle bridle. Rein contact is made with four reins. The low setting of the cavesson noseband corresponds to the dropped noseband on a bridle. The use of two sets of leather-heavy tack is only appropriate for short periods of time and to allow for the quick addition and removal of the cavesson. For longer sessions, you should forego the dropped noseband and the low-buckled cavesson.*

nose. Using a cavesson with the snaffle attached directly to it eliminates extra leather.

To fundamentally presuppose that horses must be dominated in order to be mastered is as erroneous as the supposition that they must be allowed to express every desire in order to be true to their nature. The hierarchical order in a herd is established and regulated by tough reprimands amongst herd members. Every horse is advised of his limits, and boldness is immediately curbed. Sentimental pampering of a horse in your daily dealings with him, permitting every transgression, and pointlessly feeding treats without expecting prior performance— perhaps to curtail misbehavior and bribe for

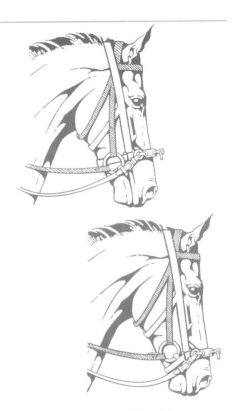

## The Cavesson with a Snaffle Bridle

*Above:* A cavesson for use under saddle with the addition of a snaffle bridle and two pairs of reins (shaded). The jowl and jawbands of the cavesson must run underneath the cheekpieces of the snaffle bridle in order to maintain the bit's sensitivity to the rein aids. The cavesson's nosepiece is adjusted over the nasal bone where the pressure effect is weak and corresponding to where the bridle's noseband would be.

*Below*: A low attachment of the cavesson's nosepiece (corresponding to the dropped noseband). The jawband runs below the snaffle bit and around the chin. The nosepiece rests on the lower part of the horse's nose where the pressure effect is more severe. This variation is not for sensitive horses and is only suitable for empathetic, responsive hands. This should not be used with the bridle's noseband, as well.

## Riding with a Cavesson

*Above:* A riding cavesson with one pair of reins and without a snaffle bridle. The "stems" of the outer rings are up to 2 1/2 inches long and point outward to the sides in order to teach the horse to bend into the turns.

*Below:* A light riding cavesson combined with an eggbutt snaffle. This is an exemplary combination for training that eliminates a lot of "leather" and protects a young horse's mouth. It is also excellent for a beginner rider on a schooled horse to learn to use four reins.

Left: *A cavesson fitted above the bit on the horse's nose. The pressure is exerted on the bony part of the nose and has a softer effect. This style corresponds to an English noseband with a bridle.*
Right: *The cavesson is attached lower, the jawband runs below the bit and around the chin, and the pressure effect on the lower part of the nose is magnified. This style corresponds to a dropped noseband. A bridle noseband, in either case, is unnecessary.*

obedience—are considered by the horse to be confirmations of his behavior and will result in aggressive begging and a general lack of respect. Though well-intended, regarding the horse as an affectionate pet with the hope that he will honor leniency, can become dangerous for the "animal lover." Because of his innate, hierarchal behavior, the horse instinctively takes advantage of man's weaknesses and flaws, at times asserting his will with some rather brusque herd manners. Man's timid and indecisive reactions allow the horse to take over the role as leader.

Only decisive, determined, and energetic leadership provided by man can prevent the horse from taking the upper hand. Horses do not deal with each other in a timid way— especially stallions that strive to lead because they are programmed to do so. Once a horse has asserted himself over his human handler, antagonism and aggression are not far behind. As a consequence, man often resorts to physical punishment, and eventually, the horse is labeled a rogue. Malicious horses are very seldom born that way; they are made that way by man. Timely intervention using maneuvers and exercises can distract the horse, awaken his desire to work, and prevent confrontations.

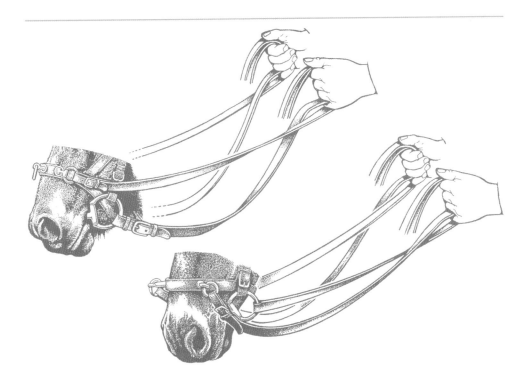

## Holding the Reins of the Snaffle-Cavesson Combination

*Above:* Holding the reins in the early stages of training the young horse when using a cavesson and a snaffle bridle without a noseband. All rein aids are given via the cavesson reins, particularly in the cases of horses with very sensitive mouths. Each hand holds one cavesson and one snaffle bridle rein. The cavesson reins, due to the protruding rings on the cavesson noseband, are always held on the outside of the snaffle reins, which run closely along the horse's neck. The cavesson reins run underneath the little finger, and the snaffle reins between the little and ring fingers into the fist; both leave the fist together between the index finger and the thumb. The ends of all four reins should hang down between the right side of the horse's neck and the right-hand reins. The little finger can exert varying pressure on the horse's nose while the snaffle reins remain uninvolved. The

cavesson noseband is fitted over the bony part of the horse's nose where the pressure effect is rather mild. Beginner riders with clumsy hands will exert little pain using the cavesson reins in this way on school horses.

*Below:* A cavesson with a snaffle bit directly attached to it—the elimination of unnecessary, abrasive, and pinching extra leather. With advanced training of the young horse, the rein aids transition smoothly, playfully, and almost unnoticeably over to the snaffle reins, and the effect of the cavesson is gradually reduced. For this reason, the rein pairs are now reversed in the hand: the cavesson reins run between the little and ring fingers, and the snaffle reins run underneath the little finger into the hands. In this manner, the little finger can now play softly with the snaffle in the horse's mouth, while the cavesson reins rather passively contribute toward maintaining the horse's bend at the poll.

# The Trainer's Body Language

In order to be understood and assert himself as the "highest ranking animal," the trainer must simulate, as closely as possible, the horse's body language. The herd leader attains respect through an impressive posture, so to emphasize his hierarchal dominance when in the horse's presence, the trainer must assume a "larger than life" stance. Even though the horse may not recognize a two-legged man as one of his own kind, he will respect familiar body language. Body posture that is bent over, crooked, or collapsed is a sign of submissiveness to the horse—as it is in the herd—and, therefore, costs the trainer respect. Superior, upright body posture with head held high (just like the herd leader exhibits) demands esteem.

This goes hand-in-hand with maintaining a measured personal space, a certain distance from the horse, as is practiced, for example, when working in hand. The trainer sustains a distance of about an arm's length so he can stay within the horse's range of vision. The horse can observe all of his movements without being able to close in on, or barge into the trainer. While longeing, the trainer can express disapproval or approval with concise gestures. If the trainer turns directly toward the horse and makes eye contact, he can confront or reject the horse's behavior; the horse will feel challenged or driven. On the other hand, when the trainer turns and looks away from the horse, he communicates conciliation, approval, and calm.

The riding arena is usually a quiet place so softly spoken words and commands capture the horse's interest. The same voice modulations should always precede physical aids, until the horse reacts to the voice signals alone. The horse will not comprehend inarticulate screaming, and sudden, surprising, aimless movements that do not accompany specific commands will not only be misunderstood by the horse, they will irritate him.

The trainer must always be conscious of "saving face." When the horse is over-faced and cannot accomplish a requested exercise, the trainer must reduce the difficulty of the request; if he insists that a task the horse cannot do be completed, he will lose authority. This is the reason for asking for small advances, not necessarily perfection, as well as avoiding numerous repetitions. The trainer needs to clearly acknowledge when the horse has satisfactorily accomplished an exercise. A cooperative attitude should be praised and rewarded, even if the performance is nowhere near an optimal result.

Observing the behavior of a herd of wild horses—their body language and their gestures—teaches a trainer about communication between man and animal. When the trainer makes extensive use of the horse's natural expressions and behavior, he will not only gain the horse's trust, he will be understood. Before obedience can be demanded, there must be a foundation of trust. The training principle is based on praise and reward. During incidents of obvious disobedience and opposition, the trainer must respond immediately with the least amount of reprimand necessary. Often, a raised voice, alone, can serve as punishment. If the punishment, particularly physical punishment, follows the act even a few minutes too late, then the horse will not understand the connection.

In summary, it must be concluded that during a young horse's training, the cavesson can prevent pain and injury to—and maintain the sensitivity of—the tongue, bars, and corners of the mouth. Also, the cavesson allows beginner riders on schooled horses to learn to hold and handle the reins without harming the horse's mouth.

Using the cavesson for work in hand requires the trainer to display body language that is both clear and similar to that of horses so his requests are understood. Specific body movements, always preceded by vocal commands, accompany and emphasize required exercises. A punishing jerk to the nose should discreetly—but immediately and energetically—follow misbehavior, without the horse considering it a threatening movement. Successful use of the cavesson requires the trainer to clarify that he is the "herd leader," and he will not tolerate disobedience and opposition. The consistent and correct use of the cavesson can provide a trainer with an animal-friendly tool to educate both horse and rider.

## Rules of Thumb for the Cavesson

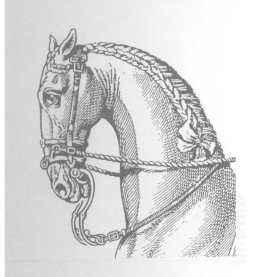

● *The cavesson should be considered universal bridling for the education and training of the horse, both in hand and under saddle, preventing pain or early damage to the horse's sensitive mouth.*

● *The iron inset that makes up the nosepiece must fit so that it does not slip. The underside of the nosepiece should consist of smooth leather without any sharp edges (for example, metal teeth or tacks).*

● *The jowl and jawbands should be padded and provide a fairly tight, preferably immovable, non-pinching fit that allows the horse to chew gently.*

● *The nosepiece should rest on the upper bony part of the nasal bridge, one to two finger-widths below the cheekbone.*

● *Both outer rings should be attached to long stems so that steering aids via contact, either through reins or a lead line, can be clearly conveyed.*

# A Foreign Object in
# the Horse's Mouth

When considering the bridle and reins, you should begin with the horse's highly sensitive mouth. The bit rests in the tooth-free spaces, called the *bars*, between the front *molars and canines*. (The canine teeth are common in stallions and geldings, but are seldom seen in mares.) The horse's front incisors serve to pick up food; pincer-like, they rip and tear grasses and weeds. The molars then grind them up, but canine teeth do not serve any function.

The bars, where the metal bit rests, are covered with thin, mucous membranes that have a high degree of circulation, many nerves, and are highly sensitive to pain and easily injured. During the time period when the young horse's teeth change (usually between his second and fourth years), natural, temporary inflammations of the gums occur. Sometimes, small teeth that are approximately one centimeter in length called *wolf teeth* grow out of the upper jaw, right in front of the first molars. These relics from ancient times do not serve a present purpose, and by growing into the bars, they may push against the bit and cause a painful reaction. The molars may wear unevenly and result in the formation of "hooks" or sharp points on their outer walls. These may injure the inner membrane of the horse's cheek when he is chewing, especially if parts of the bridle are pressing onto the cheeks from the outside. Older horses can suffer from tooth illness, long-term inflammation, and gum infection that make a bit intolerable. When, in addition to natural hardship, there is also a painful bit

*The bridle and bit must fit a horse's head like a custom-made suit.*

or brutal rein contact, the horse can easily reach a state of panic and become a risk to his rider and environment. In the long run, the horse will refuse to accept a bridle and bit, or he will ignore or resist the rider's aids because he is distracted by the pain in his mouth.

Anatomical form, individual mouth size, and length of bars can vary greatly from horse to horse. The branches of the lower jaw can be close together or far apart; they can be narrow with a sharp edge or broad and round. The tongue can be long or short, flat or thick; the palate can be flat or curved upward, and the bars can be broadly or narrowly formed.

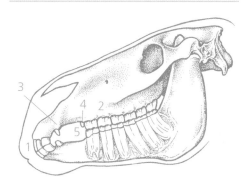

**The Skull of a Mature Horse**
① Incisors ② Molars ③ Canine Teeth ④ Wolf Teeth (found infrequently) ⑤ Bars—the tooth-free space where the bit rests

Anatomical criteria can have a positive or negative effect on rein contact. An exact evaluation of mouth construction and subsequent careful selection of bit and bridle is absolutely necessary—particularly in reference to the middle joint in the snaffle and the *port* (for tongue freedom) in the curb, both of which push against the palate and may press against the tongue. You can prevent injury to the bars and corners of the mouth by watching for worn-out snaffle rings or movable curb shanks on broken or stiff bits. And of course, the "rein hands" have the final say: they can refine the aids through soft feel or completely destroy the mouth through brutal force.

Some bits are constructed in such a way that they rest primarily on the elastic cushion of the tongue; some distribute the pressure evenly to the tongue and bars; others affect mostly the bars alone. The two branches of the lower jaw are firm, inflexible bones covered by thin membranes; the only way they can evade the pressure of the bit is by moving backward. Or, when they have been completely blunted, they resist the pressure and do not move at all. They often visibly show, therefore, the obvious traces of painful aids.

Special attention must be paid to the horse's highly sensitive tongue. This center of sensitivity demands that the rider conduct the reins with refinement and feeling—no matter what kind of bridle, bit, or style of riding. The tongue is extremely flexible: It can change its position in the horse's mouth horizontally and vertically; it can lengthen or shorten, and curve up or lie flat. The horse can evade pain from pressure by pulling his tongue back and putting it over the bit. The tongue can be rubbed sore or hurt extensively by rollers, or other gadgets, on bits.

The jointed or unjointed bit, depending on its construction, rests more or less directly on the elastic cushion of the tongue. The stronger the pull on the reins, the greater the pressure exerted on the tongue. Empathetic hands, through soft signals and little, pulsing tweeks, invite the tongue to playfully counter the pressure, resulting in an unforced dialogue. The soft conversation transmits to the rider that the horse is happy with the rein contact. The horse's tongue is squished against the lower jaw by brutal pulling on the reins, and therefore, cannot respond to the inquiring rein hand or be a partner in any conversation. The epitome of empathetic rein contact is the dialogue, conducted mostly without putting pressure on the bars, between the rider's hands and the horse's tongue.

The width of the bit must fit exactly to the corners of the horse's mouth, in order for the contact to be free from interference. The outer ends of the bit should fit the corners of the mouth so that, at the most, two wrinkles are formed. There should be almost a centimeter of extra space between the corners of the mouth and the snaffle rings on each side so the lips are not compressed or chafed. If the bit is too wide with too much room to play, then the danger exists that the lower jaw will be squeezed too much when the reins are taken up.

The less the bit feels like a foreign object, the looser and more relaxed the horse is, and the more inclined he will be to willingly respond to the rider's rein aids. Bits of a manner of constructions put different kinds of pressure on the tongue, bars, palate, and

*Above: A double-jointed snaffle bit with a copper roller—a kind, "friendly" bit. Below: A dressage curb and bradoon snaffle; the two bits fill the horse's mouth and so must be fitted precisely.*

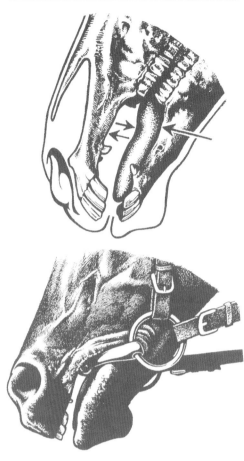

**Areas of Sensitivity in the Horse's Mouth**

*Above:* The points where the snaffle bit puts pressure on the tongue and palate (indicated by the short arrows) and bars (indicated by the long arrow) when the reins are tightened.

*Below:* The simple snaffle with one middle joint will form a triangle in the horse's mouth, pushing against the palate when the reins are taken up, particularly if the bit is too big (more than a third of an inch showing outside the horse's lips on each side). If the noseband and cavesson are buckled too snugly, the horse's mouth can't open and yield, and in combination with rough rein contact, they will intensify the pressure on the palate, tongue, and bars.

**The Horse's Tongue: The Center of Contact Sensitivity**

*Above:* A simple snaffle, jointed in the middle, becomes a triangle when the reins are taken up.

*Middle:* A double-jointed snaffle (like a KK Conrad). The middle joints align themselves with the shape of the tongue and protect the palate.

*Below:* Sometimes a horse will pull back his tongue and place it over the bit to relieve himself of painful pressure.

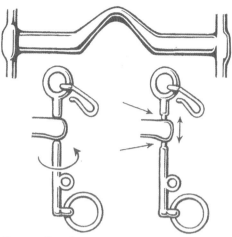

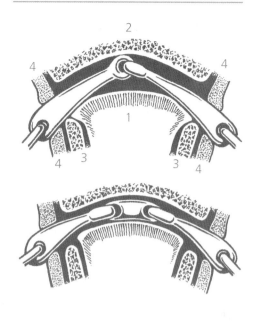

## Tongue Freedom

Because the port (the elevated space for the tongue) is too narrow, when the reins are taken up, this curb bit will push against the palate and squeeze the edges of the tongue. Curb shanks that twist or shift vertically ("sliding cheek" curbs) can wear out the drill holes of the mouthpiece and form sharp ridges that can injure the corners of the horse's mouth.

## Fitting the Snaffle Bit

*Left:* This bit is too wide; when the reins are tightened, the pinching effect on the lower jaw will increase.

*Middle:* This bit is too narrow; the horse's lips will be rubbed raw.

*Right:* A well-fitted bit; it exceeds both sides of the mouth by just under a third of an inch.

## Cross Section of a Horse's Mouth at the Bars

*Above*: The snaffle in the horse's mouth. When the reins are taken up, the single-jointed snaffle assumes the shape of a triangle, pushing upward against the palate, and pinching the lower jaw. ① Tongue ② Palate ③ Bars ④ Lips.

*Below*: The double-jointed snaffle bit. When reins are tightened and the bit is turned, it nestles against the arch of the tongue and protects the palate, limiting the pinching effect on the lower jaw.

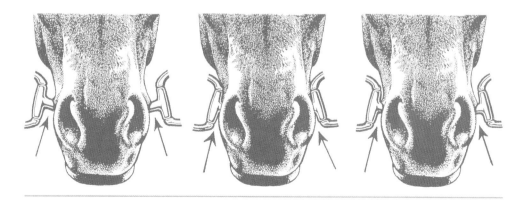

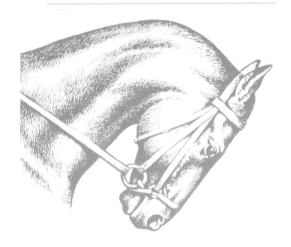

**Head Carriage Caused by Hard, Cruel Rein Contact**

*Above:* The hardened horse, with a sensitive mouth that has been dulled, leans heavily into the bridle and searches for a "fifth leg" as support.

*Below:* The horse escapes contact by going "behind the bit" in order to evade the painful pressure on his tongue and bars.

Both head and neck carriages show the false "break" at the third and fourth neck vertebrae. The highest point of the arched neck must be at the poll, right behind the ears.

corners of the mouth. Bridles of varying impact complement the bit and result in other pressure points in different areas of the horse's head, like the crown, nasal bone, chin, and lower jaw. Simple bridles (without additional mechanical aids, such as a martingale or draw reins) almost always fulfill their purpose because they establish a direct and true connection between the rider's hands and the horse's mouth, transmitting the rider's signals instantaneously and unequivocally.

Bars with sharp edges are more sensitive than those that are rounded, and with rough rein contact, the mucous membranes can be rubbed off, and the skin over the bone may become inflamed. Scar tissue may then grow over the bone, the sensitivity of the bars may decline, and the horse can develop a "hard mouth." Or, he may suffer whenever any pressure is put on the bars. As a result, bridling with a normal bit becomes nearly impossible.

While the horse is growing, it must be noted if the canine teeth do erupt (which does sometimes occur in mares) the surrounding mucous membrane often becomes temporarily inflamed, causing pain. During this time, it is advisable to use a bitless cavesson as a provisional substitute to the normal bridle. Use a thick, light, and hollow metal or soft rubber snaffle for a starter bit—it is only to accustom the horse to a bit, rather than transmitting rein aids.

For subsequent use, there are a number of basic bit and bridle constructions that have, over time, proven to inflict little pain on the horse's mouth and be fairly easy for a rider to use. In light of the undeniable existence of animal cruelty, a number of bit constructions will be discussed that are designed to cause horse's pain. Suppliers offer many variations of bits that are both friendly and cruel toward horses. Even minor changes in form can turn a mild bit into a severe one; if it does not fit the horse's anatomic make-up, it will cause discomfort.

It does not pay to use cheap products, as it may very well backfire. It is highly advisable—with the well-being of the horse and the safety of the rider in mind—to always use only first class, brand name bits made out of the best possible materials and formed with the comfort of the horse's mouth in mind. A higher price is certainly worth it when you consider the careful construction and finish, and longer lasting material that save the horse's mouth from injury and prevent accidents. Anonymously manufactured, cheap products lack the qualities of well-made bits. Their edges, corners, and seams show defective workmanship and may chafe the horse's mouth. The movable parts often wear out, and sharp ridges may form around them, creating the very real possibility of actually breaking and endangering the rider's safety. These considerations make the choice between quality and inferior products a simple one.

The *eggbutt, racing or dee ring*, and *full-cheek* snaffles are preferable to the *loose-ring snaffle* with its simple ring holes, as they protect the corners of the horse's mouth and prevent the bit from being pulled sideways through the mouth by clumsy or cruel hands. Because the recommended snaffle variations protect the corners of the mouth, and because they are provide gentle steering aids that lessen the impact of minor rein aid mistakes, they are particularly suited for

beginner riders and training young horses.

Unusual, specialty bits that should only be used by experienced, serious professionals will not be discussed at length in this book, as in the hands of the beginner—and even the more advanced rider—they are more often a hindrance (and a danger) than a help. Besides, the capable rider does not need specialty bits very often, simply because he is so capable and can, therefore, do without these aids.

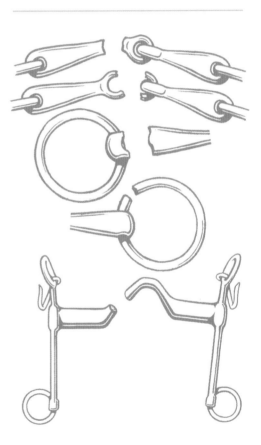

Possible Breakage Points in Cheap Bits

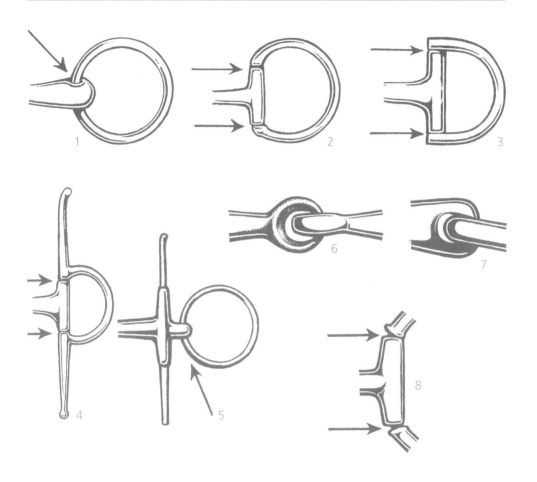

**Typical Points of Snaffle Wear and Tear**
① Loose-ring snaffle; ② eggbutt snaffle; ③ dee-ring snaffle; ④ full-cheek snaffle with solid half rings; ⑤ full-cheek snaffle with movable outer rings. The arrows indicate movable points of connection that can wear out and form sharp, hurtful ridges. The further these points are from the corners of the horse's mouth, the better. The best choice is the full-cheek snaffle with outer rings (number five) because the corners of the mouth do not come anywhere near the ring holes. ⑥ A worn-out middle joint on a snaffle: the rings get thinner where they rub together, until they break. ⑦ A worn-out ring hole on a snaffle (seen from the top of the ring); sharp ridges can damage the corners of the horse's mouth. ⑧ The most commonly seen kind of ring-hole wear; the horse's lips will be pinched.

Numerous bit types are superfluous or even damaging in their use. Very basic bit models can provide mostly pain-free influence, as long as the rider's hands are sensitive and kind. Some riders, confronted with their own limitations, are tempted to blame the horse for their inabilities and turn to forceful auxiliary aids for help. In the end, it is the rider's ability that creates successful or failed rein contact, and neither a friendly "basic" bit nor a cruel "specialty" bit can reconcile that. A straightforward, simple bit and bridle will satisfy the needs of the capable rider because he knows how to apply his independent seat, weight, and thigh aids to achieve soft and empathetic rein contact.

## Common Effects of the Bit in the Horse's Mouth

*The tongue and palate, the branches of the lower jaw (the bars), and the corners of the mouth are highly sensitive, and pressure or chafing from bits and rough rein contact can cause serious injury, creating an unresponsive mount.*

- *The middle of the tongue feels pressure from the middle joint of the snaffle (be it single or double) at the pivotal moment when the reins are picked up.*

- *The edges of the tongue are squeezed by the two arms of the snaffle when the bit forms a triangle in the horse's mouth, and even more so if a curb with a too-narrow port is used.*

- *The palate feels pressure from a single-jointed snaffle at the pivot moment when the reins are taken up and the bit forms a triangle and also from a curb with a high port.*

- *The bars experience chafing and pressure from both snaffle and curb bits when the rider takes up the reins.*

- *The corners of the mouth are pinched by worn-out bit parts with movable suspensions, especially loose-ring snaffles and curbs with shanks that revolve or shift vertically.*

# The Rider's Hands and the Response from the Horse's Mouth

*The play between the hands and the horse's mouth is similar to a conversation between friends.*

The principle behind a rider's rein contact is often misunderstood and, consequently, practiced incorrectly. Often, the horse experiences pain, and in despair, he withdraws from or actively opposes the aids. The goal of achieving harmony between horse and rider is not attained, and the "tough" horse is blamed. The rider's weaknesses, commonly the actual cause of problems, are seldom discussed. Other problems include the inadequate and forceful training methods used when commercial interests take precedence over what is best for the horse—the horse often becomes dull and mechanical, or tense and performs out of fear.

The horse, by nature, is a flight animal, and the forward urge is his life-preservation instinct. The mechanics for the gaits develop out of the hind end, and that is why it is only natural that collection should develop there as well, from the back to the front. At first, the horse considers the way the rein aids limit

*The Spanish walk: Commendable, soft rein contact, without the faults of a false "lifting" rein or allowing the hindquarters to drag.*

his forward drive a nonsensical hindrance, until he understands how to measure the sequence of his gaits and balance the equilibrium he now shares with the rider. He learns to translate forward thrust into carrying power and shorten and raise his steps. In the first basic segment of training, the variation between aids that drive and those that limit regulates the horse's forward thrust, tempo, and gait sequence. It is important that restrictive rein aids are not given at the same time the hind legs push off. The half-halt is used before the hind foot sets down, and the reins are released when the hind foot leaves the ground again, encouraging impulsion.

In advanced stages of training, on the other hand, the rein aids create a frame, strengthen the carrying power of the hindquarters, and support and encourage the upright carriage and rounded body posture that allows the rider to swing along on an arched, elastic back.

**The Principle of Forward-driving and Form-giving Aids**

*Above left:* In the passage, the thrust from the hindquarters moves primarily forward (indicated by arrow).

*Above right:* In the piaffe, the thrust of the hindquarters develops upward from the bent hocks, strengthening carrying power (see the arrow) and molding the horse into a compressed and rounded spring.

*Forward-driving and Form-giving Aids in the Training Stage*
*Below left: Forward-driving aids in the trot extension exhibit a
primarily forward direction of thrust.*
*Below: Form-giving aids in the piaffe: The rein contact directs the
thrust upward and transforms it into carrying power. The horse's
profile remains in front of the vertical, and the horse's neck is not
restricted. This is commendable rein contact. With advanced
gymnasticizing of the hocks, the hind feet will step further under the
horse's body, the croup will lower, the hindquarters will carry more
weight, and the head and neck will become more upright.*

# The Horse's Balance

In the natural sequence of the gaits, without a rider's influence, the horse moves in a more or less balanced manner, though seldom in a straight line (similar to man himself). Often, the horse will step one hind hoof off the track in order to counter-balance momentary lateral unsteadiness, or he will vary the length of his stides or the tempo in order to "catch" longitudinal instabilities. The faster the tempo and the gait, the less frequently moments of lost equilibrium occur because forward impulsion stabilizes balance, as you experience when riding a bicycle.

As soon as the rider occupies the horse's back, the horse must learn to rebalance himself with the additional, swaying burden, especially if he is carrying an inexperienced rider. In order to imagine what this might be like, think of carrying a restless child on your shoulders and trying to walk. Not only do you have to consider your own imbalance, but you must also reconcile the child swinging forward, backward, and to the side as you try to step under your shared center of gravity. As a result, your steps inevitably become smaller and more cautious.

Despite the fact that he has four legs, the horse has similar problems finding his center of gravity with an additional burden on his back, particularly when he is further disturbed by a rider's lack of balance. Consequently, the rider must literally "aid" the horse in stabilizing himself. He should sit perpendicular to the horse's back at the center of gravity, without leaning forward or backward. He should correct lateral imbalances by driving the horse into a studious forward gait, bringing him onto a straight line. The horse should neither step wide behind, nor fall sideways off the track in the front. A rider who leans forward or backward with his upper body, or whose head falls forward, will disturb the horse's equilibrium, and his aids will be ineffective. The balance of the rider also depends on his anatomical body build. For example, the horse is better able to cope with a rider with a short upper body than a long one.

As the musculature of the hindquarters strenthens, collection is developed from the back to the front, until self-carriage is attained. The level of the head and neck carriage—that is, the height at which the head and neck are positioned—must correspond to the level of the horse's training. The neck must not be shortened or confined, nor must the muscles under the neck bulge. The line of the forehead must remain in front of the vertical. The forced, active raising of the head restricts the neck, the muscles under the neck bulge out, the neck and back musculature tightens, and the rider is bounced in the trot. The "arched bow" outline of the horse is disturbed. The term *relative* head and neck carriage refers to the position that the horse offers without being forced by the reins. On the other hand, *active* head and neck carriage is artificially derived from intervening hands that do not remain passive.

The body posture of a stallion running free, his impressive trot full of suspension, teaches the rider, by example, how the horse finds his balance with a relaxed head and neck carriage. Under the rider, the head and neck carriage must remain just as relaxed and must not be restricted by strong flexing at the poll.

*Early in training, the young horse must find his balance
under the unaccustomed weight of the rider. He is
supported in this effort by careful, passive rein contact
on a long rein that should not interfere or disturb this
precarious balance.*

**Relative versus Active Raising of the Horse's Head and Neck**

*Above:* A natural, *relative*, and unforced raising of the head and neck is offered by the horse—it should correspond to his level of training. The hind legs assume more weight and, in relation to the degree of hindquarter engagement, the head and neck will be raised proportionately.

*Below right:* A forced, *active* raising of the head and neck where the top of the neck shows a false "break," the muscles under the neck are bulging out, and the hind legs are not stepping far enough under the body or taking on more weight.

# The Horse's Head Movement

In the free, unrestricted walk the horse lowers his head when he swings one of his front legs forward; the moment the front leg touches down on the ground, the horse lifts his head, lowering it again as the other front leg swings forward, and so on. This "nodding" head movement, like a pendulum in the rhythm of forward-swinging legs, has a balancing effect—similar to the swing of a man's arms when he is walking. When beginning work with a young horse, the rider's reins must not interfere with the horse's free walk and nodding head. At first, the rider's hands must foster the nodding and forward momentum of the walk so the horse can come to terms with the added weight of the rider in his search for balance. Confining rein contact inhibits the forward movement, limits the freedom of the shoulder, and invites resistance. The rider should encourage the head movement by yielding the reins and moving each hip and shoulder forward in harmony with each hind leg. Later, in a more advanced training stage, when the strength of the musculature has increased, "throughness" at the poll, and a relaxed, quiet head and neck carriage have been achieved, then the rider may gradually limit—and later strongly restrict—the nodding movement. Finally, in collected self-carriage with very soft rein contact, the movement will disappear completely as the horse has learned through gymnastic exercise to maintain his balance and equilibrium with his muscle strength.

*An example of relative head and neck carriage. The body posture of the ridden horse does not differ from the free-running stallion. The rein contact is carefully adapted to the natural head and neck carriage at the extended trot.*

*In the free, strolling walk on a long rein, the horse displays the unimpeded nodding head movement, like a balancing pendulum, and similar to man's swinging arms when he walks.*

During the horse's early learning phase, the active rein takes on the primitive function of braking. The hands pull on the reins in order to halt the horse, his head bends backward, and he stops. The rein is then yielded immediately as a reward. At first, the rider does not drive with his body but adapts passively, without intervention, to the movement of the horse. As the training advances, the rider gradually begins to use driving aids that are in harmony with the now lessening rein aids. The horse should carry the bit on his tongue and bars and search for contact. The hands become passive, maintain a sensitive connection, and do not disturb him.

After completed training, the head and neck show relative upright carriage with a relaxed, stretched neck and without forced rein contact. The head is carried quietly and does not nod because the horse has learned to balance himself with muscle strength alone. The powerful thrust from the hindquarters is caught and guided by a gentle, almost unnoticeable rein contact; rein aids are now merely soft reminders. The rider sits upright, and his hands are held absolutely quietly and passively. Without tightening the muscles in his lower back or depending on his strength, the rider uses a slight rotation of his upper body and, if necessary, gliding rein hands (a yielding outside rein and a "taking" inside rein) to transmit turns, and the horse chews happily, his mouth closed. The rider should never pull on the inside rein without yielding the outside rein, as then the forward thrust is blocked and the turning effect eliminated.

In exceptional cases, as for example, in the canter when the horse pushes his head

**The Beginnings of Collection**
The uncollected horse carries his head and neck in the natural position with soft rein contact; his hind legs do not carry more weight, and due to a lack of bend in the hocks, there is no lowering of the croup. The horse is moving in a ground-covering, working trot. He is altogether loose and relaxed; the rider does not interfere, he merely adapts to the movement without disturbing the horse.

downward in order to grab the reins out of the rider's hands, it is advisable to use energetic tugs on the reins as an emergency tool so that the horse does not take over as leader of your "herd." In order to be effective, the pressure on the reins must hold fast against the beginning phase of the canter, and then the reins must immediately be released so the horse does not set himself against the hands, and so every other canter stride is not blocked in its inception.

*A half-halt at the canter in order to bring the forward- and downward-leaning horse under control. When necessary, the half-halt blocks the horse's hind legs as they push off and the rider's forward-driving seat in order to achieve a "braking" effect. The hindquarters push forward under the body, the front end lifts, and the horse becomes more "through." The direction of movement, which earlier aimed at the ground, is now aimed upward. The predominant aid is the rider's driving seat, which gathers the hindquarters.*

# The Rider's Leadership

From the beginning of his education, the young horse becomes accustomed to the rein aids and, therefore, to the leadership of the rider. This is accomplished by using the cavesson and snaffle with four reins, which also protects the mouth and maintains its sensitivity.

Communication with the horse's mouth via the rein aids exerts varying pressure on the lower jaw and consists of a variety of finely differentiated "plucks" that flow into one another, from one or both reins. They may be a gentle call to attention before an upcoming turn, or they may ask for a full halt, but either way, they must be followed by an immediate yielding of the hands, or they may result in opposing pressure from the horse's mouth. In the beginning, at the walk, the young horse considers a holding hand particularly restrictive—a braking force—and, therefore, he should be allowed to carry his head and neck unrestrained in a natural and relaxed position. There should only be a very light and variable rein connection that does not hold back but rather fosters cautious leadership and permits free, uninhibited forward strides.

The young horse begins with simple changes of direction, from straight to "broken" or looped lines; later, different school figures present various turns, circles, and lateral movements. When introducing turns, the beginner rider commits the most common error: he pulls the horse's head into the turn with the inner rein and forgets to yield with the outer rein correspondingly. As a result, the horse's head is tilted (crooked in the poll), his mouth receives contradictory pressure, and the sequence of the gaits is

*A trot half-pass to the right. Lateral movements gymnasticize the longitudinal bending of the horse on both sides and eliminate natural crookedness. The rein contact remains the same on both sides.*

disturbed. The rider should always yield the outer rein in a turn, while keeping the inner rein unchanged or shortening it only a little. Generally, the inner rein should only be shortened by as much as the outer rein is yielded, so that both corners of the horse's mouth experience the same contact, and the horse continues to feel both reins. Thus, turns are indicated through the parallel gliding of the hands: the outer hand goes forward as the inner hand, at the same time, goes backward.

With advanced training, the rein aids should be reduced and the aid system should gradually be transferred from the hands to the energetically driving seat and influence of the thighs. It is important that the rein aids do not counteract the seat and thighs. A rider should not contain a horse that has an excessive forward urge with forceful reins; rather, he should use longitudinal bending in the lateral movements to do so. This will prevent the horse from becoming "tight" in the neck. Frequent riding of various school figures is good practice for seamless transitions between the driving and containing aids. It is important to remember that longitudinal bending must always take place throughout the horse's entire body, in order to be effective. The bending of the neck alone will not make the horse look like a horizontal "tensed bow" from head to tail, if seen from above.

Containing aids meant to regulate the gaits must be applied at the correct moment in the gait's sequence so the horse understands the aid. Most of the time, the containing aid should occur during the hind leg's forward swing, immediately yielding when the other hind leg pushes off and allowing the forward thrust to continue, unimpeded. Only in circumstances where the tempo is to be greatly reduced should a half-halt occur at the moment the hind leg thrusts off the ground. However, it must be remembered that the seat and thigh aids always have priority over the rein aids. If the horse is obedient to the half-halt, then the pressure on the reins must be immediately released. Should the horse not obey, then the half-halts must be repeated at short intervals until the desired gait regulation is achieved.

Effective handling of the reins is only possible once the horse is "through," that is, when the horse can—without longitudinal effort—bend on both sides throughout his entire body and when he can, by stepping under his body with his hind legs, master the vertical "tensed bow" from head to tail, if seen from the side. At that point, the rein aids can successfully affect the horse from his mouth to his hindquarters, and vice versa.

Collected exercises requiring extensive bending of the hocks, like the piaffe, cause the hindquarters to tense, shorten, and lower themselves; to the same degree, the forehand must loosen and relax in its upright carriage. When the head and neck are confined and the rein aids act in a backward manner, the horse restrains his movement and evades the bit, going behind the vertical. In this case, the half-halt is not communicated. *Durchlaessigkeit*, or "throughness," is difficult to achieve because the horse wants to avoid strenuously bending his hocks, and so he will bump against or crawl behind the bit, causing the holding rein aids to become ineffective. The pushing power of the hindquarters must be allowed to fully unfold, developing forward and upward; it must not be restricted

**Yielding Rein Contact**
In collection—for example, in the piaffe—the rein contact must be yielded (indicated by arrow) to the same degree as the hindquarters are tensed, bent, and lowered, allowing the horse's head and neck relaxed freedom and an upward carriage so that the horse is able to balance himself on a smaller base. The less the rider intervenes with the reins, and the more supplely he sits at the center of gravity, the easier it will be for the horse to find a shared balance.

by the reins. The hands must allow an upright carriage of the horse's head and neck, and then cautiously contain it so the "throughness" is maintained from the back to the front.

# Rein Contact

An independent "deep seat" at the center of gravity and the lowest point of the horse's back, perfectly balanced, upright, with an erect head posture and without a collapsed waist, is the prerequisite for successful empathetic rein contact. The connection negotiated between the horse's mouth and the rider's hands must remain alive and uninterrupted so that the rider controls the horse and not the other way around. The only exception is when the reins are given forward freely, either as a reward for an accomplished task or for a relaxed stroll with a long neck. The rider's hands and wrists must remain supple in order to give multiple, refined aids at any time and prevent cramping or tightness.

The basis for communicating with the horse through the reins is *contact*, that is, the steady, light connection between the rider's hands and the horse's mouth. The bit of the bridle rests on the tongue and bars, and the horse's mouth should remain closed, the lower jaw chewing quietly and searching—along with the sensitive, elastic tongue—for the feel of the bit. The motion of the chewing muscles, in turn, leads to the formation of saliva and foam, and transfers to the muscles at the back of the horse's neck, relaxing the whole neck. Force-free contact is only possible when the back of the neck and the jowl remain relaxed and flexible. Unrestricted longitudinal bending at the poll then becomes possible. The light alternating holding and yielding rein aids maintain soft contact with the cushion of the tongue and invite the horse's mouth to voluntarily seek connection. Yielding rein contact ensures that the horse does not lean on the bit but instead carries himself, as he should. As the horse's education is furthered, the rein contact lightens. The ultimate in self-carriage occurs when, in piaffe or passage, the rider can completely give the reins, and the horse continues in the same carriage as before, guided only by the rider's seat and thighs.

The more powerful driving aids should always exist in balance with lighter rein contact. Exaggerated driving aids against tight, restraining hands will overtax the horse and destroy balance, the "braking" rein aids forcefully inhibiting the forward momentum. The rein connection must not become stiff or tight, which would cause the horse to respond with counter pressure or by going behind the vertical and evading contact altogether. The amount of contact should vary constantly so the horse does not lean on the bit but instead answers by chewing softly. Aids and exercises during a horse's training should also vary so that the horse does not become accustomed to the same routine, day after day, and begin to anticipate aids and figures.

At times, the rider may momentarily hold the reins to the extent that the horse's face goes behind the vertical. This strong flexion, which is uncomfortable for the horse, should only be employed for good reason as a reprimand or rebuke. In contrast, simultaneously driving and holding are contradictory aids that cancel each other out, a nonsensical effect that destroys impulsion. After the beginning training phase involving the longeing cavesson, both the young horse (under the experienced trainer) and the beginner rider (on a schooled horse) should continue their education with a simple snaffle bridle without a noseband. This ensures that

*Relative and Active Rein Contact with a Snaffle Bridle without a Noseband*
*Left: Light rein contact in the passage. The horse's mouth remains closed, despite busy chewing (foam has formed on the sides of his mouth). The horse is relaxed and carries his head freely and naturally. Exemplary relative rein contact is exhibited. Right: Active contact, here in the piaffe, fosters rein contact that is too tight, and the horse's neck is constricted. However, the mouth remains closed, and the highly gymnasticized and elastic horse tolerates the strong rein contact.*

the horse's mouth is not bound together, thus restricting chewing activity, and that the rider can practice the refined feel for rein contact. The *dropped* noseband, especially, limits the chewing activity of the lower jaw and prevents the opening of the horse's mouth, as well as sometimes disguising "hard" hands. When this noseband is buckled too tightly, breathing is restricted and chewing activity is hindered. This type of force causes the chewing muscles to tense, often resulting in tongue and mouth problems, as well as tightness in the neck and back musculature.

A bridle without a noseband, however, permits the horse unrestricted chewing activity and betrays whether the rider is employing the reins empatheticly or whether he is using force, which will cause the horse to open his mouth in order to escape the pressure. When a young or beginner rider is taught on a schooled horse, right from the start he can learn to feel the horse's chewing activity and playing tongue. On the other hand, in the later stages of training when correct rein contact has been mastered, a fairly loosely-buckled noseband can be of some use, as it provides the lower jaw support against the pressure of the reins, as well as distributing that pressure slightly to the bridge of the nose through the jawband.

When, without a noseband, the horse "visibly" chews, slightly opening and closing his mouth in rhythm with the chewing activity, and when he playfully seeks contact with the bit without leaning, they should be considered positive signs of looseness and relaxation of the chewing musculature. If, on the other hand, the horse consistently has his mouth open because the reins are taut and squeezing the tongue against the lower jaw, thus preventing chewing, then there is a serious flaw in the rein contact, causing tightness in the chewing musculature and preventing a relaxed head and neck carriage. Sporadic and visible chewing in an otherwise closed mouth indicates harmony with the contact and demonstrates a sensitive and yielding rein connection.

A horse that is "through." The gymnasticized, "through" horse accepts stronger contact without opening his mouth, even when ridden without a noseband. Because the horse's ability to chew is unrestricted, the rider is able to feel and learn about sensitive rein contact.

*The passage in a snaffle bridle with a dropped noseband. In demanding exercises, the strap encircling the mouth can support the lower jaw.*

In the development of collection, the rein contact, in combination with the preceding and predominating driving aids and the increased "stepping under" of the hind legs, support the horse. The horse is pushed from the back to the front, upward into the secondary rein aids, and the forward thrust is, thus, "caught," sculpting the horse's body into a rounded, "steel spring." The pressure from the rein contact is primarily on the bars and tongue. In order to reduce the pressure to the bony, rigid bars and prevent them from becoming permanently dull to feeling, with advanced training, the rider with sensitive hands should gradually transfer the rein aids—consisting of light "plucks"—to the elastic corners of the mouth and tongue. In this manner, the painless nerve reflexes that should have precedence in the whole aid system are activated and employed, sparing the horse pressure on his bars.

When the horse's training is completed, the rein contact becomes visibly lighter. The

In the piaffe, the horse is driven from the back to the front, upward into the rein aids, which are secondary to the driving aids.

The highest level of collection in the piaffe with yielding reins. Even without rein contact, this horse demonstrates the rounded, "flexed bow" ideal, from head to hind hooves, without "falling apart." The freely carried head and neck balance the diagonal leg pairs at the smaller base, and the horse carries himself. This is an example of exemplary aids. In the piaffe, the forward momentum that serves as a stabilizer is missing, like the bicyclist who falls over when he is not going forward. Consequently, the horse has to make up for the lack of momentum with muscle power. Horses that move forward in the piaffe are searching for their balance.

horse carries his head and neck in a relaxed manner in front of the vertical and is balanced under the rider: he carries himself. He rarely leans on the reins for support, and if he does, it is with less intensity because he has learned to carry the rider's weight with his hindquarters. Ultimate collection is demonstrated especially in the piaffe: The croup lowers, giving the appearance that the horse's front end is lifted. The force-free rein connection allows the head and neck to be upright in a relaxed manner, contributing to the balanced equilibrium. Since the area in which a horse piaffes is very small and only two feet are on the ground at a time, the balance of the diagonal supports is relatively insecure. Through intervening rein aids, the rider can either support or disrupt this balance. In the piaffe, the rider's balanced seat should present the essential aids, and the rein aids should be reduced to a minimum.

For the experienced rider who has mastered the independent seat and soft, sensitive rein contact, the question of which bridle and bit to use is of little importance. Refined, sensitive hands are a match for any horse's mouth and can use nearly every bridle without causing harm. It is this rider's desire for the bit to rest on the soft cushion of the horse's tongue, rather than burden the bars. He knows that tight reins press the bit onto the bars, where metal meets bone without a cushioning buffer in between. The horse's resulting mouth-pain prohibits harmonious rein contact. The elastic tongue, on the other hand, allows the bit to spring back softly—unless hard hands are pressing it against the lower jaw.

# Mouth Problems

Horses that have not yet found their balance with the addition of a rider, or horses that do not have very sensitive mouths, tend to lean on the bit, sometimes from the start of training. They do this in order to stabilize themselves by letting the rider's hands carry their heads and necks. Often, this is caused by a lack of gymnasticizing and strengthening of the hindquarters and back muscles. The horse's hind legs do not extend far enough under his body and are too weak to carry the rider's weight. The sequence of his gaits is uncertain and wavering, and his steps are short and stomping as he struggles to find his balance. This horse pushes against the reins, trying to lengthen his neck and use it, and his head, as a balancing rod. Like a bicyclist, the horse searches for balance by thrusting forward and speeding up, running forward with quick, short steps. Then, the rider uses force to pull the horse into a flexed position, usually behind the vertical. The horse fights back against this pulling, and the rider is bounced on the horse's tense back. Thus, the spiral of pressure and counter-pressure escalates.

In order to avoid the strenuous task of stepping well under himself or bending his hocks, the horse will push himself along, trailing with his hind legs, or escape into short-and-hurried or long-and-lazy steps. He resists rein contact with one of several actions: opening his mouth; laying his tongue over the bit and letting it hang out the side of his mouth; rattling the bit impatiently or biting it; tilting his poll or going behind the vertical to escape the pressure; or leaning on the bit for support, making refined and varying rein contact completely ineffective. Sometimes, he may grind his teeth (rubbing his molars against each other) as an expression of his despair. These should all be considered symptoms of asking too much of a horse or faulty rein contact.

Either hard, forceful hands, or great sensitivity on the part of the horse's mouth, can cause a horse to pull his tongue over the snaffle in order to escape pressure. Shortening the cheekpieces of the bridle and raising the bit so it sits on the tongue, directly in front of the molars, pulls up the corners of the mouth, puts pressure on the poll, and leads the horse to clamp onto the bit—but *does not* improve the situation. Another common attempt to alleviate this problem, the use of "tongue-stretching" bits, does not solve the problem either because the cause remains the rein contact. The softer and more sensitive the rein contact is, the more relaxed the horse is and the more willing he is to respond to the rider's aids.

To the horse, the bit and bridle represent restriction of his mouth; this is amplified when a rider becomes "busy" with the reins. Control of gait sequence and direction are interventions in which the rein aids should have a *supportive* role. Even when the horse is standing with long, looped reins, the bit is a foreign object in his mouth and threatens pain once the reins are taken up. The horse submits to the bit in order to relieve himself of the possibility of pain. The functions of rein contact are steering and half-halting. As far as dressage training is concerned, the contact should be refined and without force—a playful dialogue between the questioning rider's hands and the responsive horse's mouth—and it should never "seesaw" the horse's head behind the vertical.

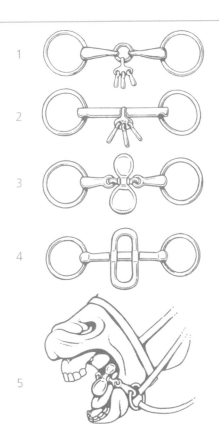

**Reprehensible Snaffle Bits**
①–② Jointed and unjointed snaffle bits with "toys" for the tongue. The little pendants are to encourage the tongue to play instead of pulling back and going over the bit. These bits do not remedy the real reason for a horse putting his tongue over the bit: hard hands and the pain they can inflict.
③–⑤ Double-jointed and unjointed snaffles with "tongue stretchers." When the reins are tightened, pressure is spread to a large surface of the tongue, pressing it against the lower jaw. These bits are also intended to prevent the tongue from going over the bit. This instrument of force does not solve the problem, is torturous for the horse, and prevents a sensitive dialogue from occurring between the rider's hands and the horse's mouth.

## Corrective Measures for Tongue Evasions

- *Use a bridle and cavesson combination with an unbroken, soft rubber or straight plastic snaffle and four reins.*

- *For an extended period, the tongue should not be pressured in order for the horse to forget the tongue pain that caused the evasion.*

- *Rein contact should only come from the cavesson reins for the time being.*

## Corrective Measures for Leaning on the Bit

- *Strengthen the horse's carrying power through gymnastic exercises for the hindquarters (exercises in hand to encourage hock bend, hill work on light inclines), and constantly vary holding and immediately yielding rein aids, lengthening periods of yielding in order to discourage leaning.*

- *Use stronger driving aids, vary the tempo of gaits, do lateral work to encourage engagement and upward carriage, and remind your horse of your constant presence by encouraging chewing activity.*

- *Varying exercises are used to distract the horse from leaning until he eventually gives it up when he finds his balance.*

## Corrective Measures for Teeth Grinding

- *Clearly lower demands and expectations, avoid any kind of force or auxiliary aid, and use sensitive rein contact.*

- *The causes are manifold and much patience is required.*

When leading a bridled horse on foot, you always have to deal carefully with his sensitive mouth. You should walk at the horse's left shoulder and optically maximize your driving effect by being behind his eye. A long whip, held in the left hand and pointing in the direction of the near hock, can increase the driving effect with horses that are lazy walkers. Your right fist should hold both reins, separating them with the index and middle fingers. The outer rein should be a little shorter so that the horse is positioned, as well as steered, slightly to the right and does not step on your feet. The right hand should hold the reins at least a foot away from the horse's mouth (not taut, but yielding) so not to disturb the nodding movement of the horse's head and to provide a rein reserve should he suddenly shy and jump to the side. In a stable or an enclosed riding arena, the remaining loop of the rein can also be held by the right hand so it does not drag on the ground. If you are leading the horse outside, or anytime you are leading a stallion, you should hold the end of the reins with the left hand. Then, if the horse makes a sudden leap or rears up, you can give with the reins without having them pulled out of one hand, allowing the horse to gallop off. In an emergency, should the right hand have to let go, both hands can grasp the rein at the buckle and hold on.

**Leading the Horse In Hand**
*The outer rein is held somewhat shorter than the inner rein so that the horse's movement is directed outward, and he will not step on the leader's feet. Both reins are carried in the right hand, with their ends running either back into the right hand or, particularly with jumpy horses, into the left hand, for safety reasons. In emergencies, the reins can be let out to their full length without being let go altogether.*

## Holding the Reins

The hands and arms of the rider should be completely loose and relaxed: his upper arms should hang vertically; his elbows should rest at his hips; and his lower arms should form a straight line with the reins so he can hold or yield at any time. The rider must not allow the horse to pull his arms forward, but instead, he must keep them at a right angle so he has enough room to yield the reins— for example, when allowing the horse to stretch forward and downward. Complex rein contact that functions independently of the rider's fluctuating seat must be practiced. Quiet hands that follow the movements of the horse's head without giving up the balanced connection are most desirable. When the horse's head and neck are quiet and straight, the hands can focus on the chewing activity of the lower jaw and the elasticity of the

**Holding the Reins on Foot**
When leading a horse in hand, allow at least a foot of rein to accommodate the nodding movement of the horse's head so he does not receive a jolt in the mouth with every step. The remainder of the reins can be looped in the leading hand.

tongue, feeling for the slightest resistance. To educate the rein hands to feel the subtlest pressure, temporarily hold the reins between index finger and thumb, keeping the hand open; in this way the activity in the horse's mouth will transmit like a seismograph to the fingers.

The snaffle bridle reins run inner-side-up, between the little fingers and ring fingers into the fists, and exit between the index fingers and the thumbs. The thumbs rest roof-like on top of the reins. The buckle should hang down between the right side of the horse's neck and the right rein. The rider differentiates and variably measures out the aids by turning the reins inward, tipping, lifting, or lowering them, moving the reins apart or pressing them together, as well as by opening his hands slightly. This varying rein pressure is transferred to the horse's mouth through stronger or lighter signals. Experienced riders with practiced hands

employ rein aids that change, depending on the aptitude and disposition of the horse, requirements of the exercises, or necessary corrections. So, for example, the reins could just as well run from the top, down between the index fingers and thumbs, into the fists, and out below. For the well-versed rider, rein methodology is not a rigid dogma but is instead dependent on the requirements of the training.

In dressage, leather reins that slide easily through the hands and allow refined degrees of tautness are used. For riding cross-country, webbed reins are useful because, though they slide through your hands fairly easily when dry, they still provide a solid grip when wet. Webbed reins with leather hand stops are not advisable as they do not allow for the necessary hand sliding and adjustment in rein length and can lead to hard, rough hands.

The snaffle bit is flexible in almost every direction. The movement of each of its parts

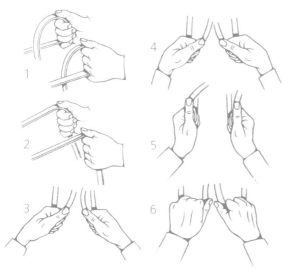

**Holding the Reins with a Snaffle Bit**

*Left:* ① The standard way to hold the snaffle reins. ② A corrective way to hold the reins during the training stage when you want to raise the horse's head and neck. The snaffle reins run between the index finger and the thumb into the rein hands. ③ The correct way to hold the reins: the wrists remain loose and supple, and the hands constantly correspond with the horse's mouth.

*Right:* Incorrect ways of holding the reins: Diagrams ④ and ⑤ depict stiff wrists with strongly bent lines to the lower arms. In ⑥, the hands are held flat instead of upright, which is called "piano hands." All of these prevent relaxed rein contact.

presents communication possibilities with the horse's mouth, and therefore, it requires a steady and light connection with the hands so the bit lies solidly and steadily on the horse's tongue, and the rein aids are clear and comprehensible. Chewing relaxes and exercises the jowl, as well as inducing the salivary gland to produce more saliva. The jowl becomes more elastic, permitting more bend at the poll.

The snaffle is the optimal bit for one- and two-sided rein aids that, along with the preceding seat and thigh aids, initiate turns, support longitudinal bending and lateral movement, and lead to the "flexed bow" of collection. Snaffle reins are attached directly to the bit and transmit the signals from the rider's hands to the tongue and bars. When the rider employs sensitive rein contact, the flexibility of the bit allows the horse's tongue to maneuver it into a comfortable position. Consequently, the horse is more willing to accept the foreign object in his mouth rather than perceive it as an object of force. The dialogue between the hands and the horse's mouth through the snaffle bit must not be disrupted. There must always be some connection. Otherwise, if the hands are "quiet," and the horse does not receive any instructions or suggestions, he will not know what the rider wants and may follow his own inclinations—the rider then loses authority.

How the hands affect the horse's mouth via the snaffle bit becomes clear when compared to the curb bit. With the curb, the effects of the hands are strengthened dramatically because the shanks and curb chain provide leverage. The hands have an indirect, more powerful effect on the horse's mouth through the lever mechanism. This mechanical effect is amplified by the rigid, unjointed, and largely immovable curb bit that does not adapt itself to the anatomy of the horse's mouth as much as a flexible snaffle. Consequently, the curb does not allow for rein aids as refined and as variably measured out as the snaffle. Therefore, the rigid curb mouthpiece is supplemented by a supple bradoon snaffle, and both together form a unit known as the *dressage double bridle*.

## Snaffle Bits

The most useful snaffle bits are characterized by mouthpieces with either single or double joints. The *single-jointed* snaffle has a more severe effect on the horse's mouth than the *double-jointed* one. When a snaffle bit is damaged or does not fit well, it can cause significant harm to a horse's mouth, possibly making it dull and insensitive, or "hard." Forceful, seesawing hands that pull the horse's head behind the vertical cause the horse much pain. When the reins are shortened, the arms of the single-jointed snaffle are bent, forming a triangle in the horse's mouth: the joint pressing against the palate and the "arms" pressing against the lower jaw, with a pinching effect. The middle joint of the bit pushes painfully against the palate (especially when the noseband is buckled very tightly), the sides of the tongue are squeezed, the thin-skinned bars are chafed until they are sore and infected, and the corners of the mouth are rubbed sore. The pinching effect is increased when the snaffle bit is too wide, exceeding the corners of the mouth by more than a third of an inch.

Conversely, if the bit is too narrow, the corners of the mouth are squeezed and rubbed sore.

Snaffle bits with integrated double joints, like the *KK Conrad* bits, are the most horse-friendly snaffle construction because, due to their form, they adapt to the anatomical roundness of the horse's tongue, their joints do not push against the palate, and the arms do not pinch the bars to any extent. Hinged snaffles with double joints, for example, the *Dr. Bristol* snaffles, are less horse-friendly because the narrow edges of the protruding middle pieces can press painfully into the tongue and palate when the reins are tightened, consequently changing the bit's angle. Double-jointed snaffles with round, copper middle pieces are well accepted by some horses because of their sweet-sour taste. When the reins are tightened, the snaffle glides back on the tongue a little, while

*The sensitive corners of the mouth have to be protected against worn-out, loose-ring snaffles by constantly checking the corners of the horse's mouth, as well as the bits. Sometimes, rubber bit guards are used with loose-ring snaffles for protection against worn-out ring holes or in order to achieve the steering effect of a dee-ring snaffle. Dried rubber, however, can chafe the sides of the mouth, especially when a bit is too narrow. Choosing a wider bit with room for bit guards is not advisable because the pinching effect on the lower jaw is increased when the reins are tightened. The disadvantages of rubber bit guards outweigh their advantages; the eggbutt, dee-ring, and full-cheek snaffles serve a far better purpose and are much friendlier to the horse's mouth.*

at the same time, it rotates forward slightly so that the underside of the bit presses on the tongue, rather than the back side (as when the bit is at rest with the reins slack). The middle piece should not be thicker than the arms of the bit so that the pressure on the tongue remains fairly constant and there are no pressure points, whatever the position of the bit may be. The integrated piece of the double-jointed KK Conrad snaffle fulfills this requirement and guarantees consistent and even pressure in every position.

The double-jointed variation of the full cheek snaffle bit is the most comfortable of all snaffles for the horse's mouth—in addition to allowing the rider very refined rein contact. This type of bit, with solidly attached shanks and movable outer rings, offers the optimal

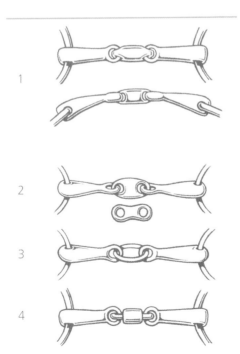

### Double-jointed Snaffle Bits

① A snaffle bit with an integrated middle piece (for example, the KK Conrad) seen from the front and below. The middle piece and joints flow smoothly into the arms and rest flat on the tongue without any pressure points, even when the angle is changed. There is only soft pressure on the tongue and bars, and there isn't any pressure on the palate. At this time, this is the most comfortable and pain-free bit—even in uneducated hands—that is available.

② A Dr. Bristol bit: the middle metal plate rests flat on the tongue when the reins are looped, but when the reins are taken up, its now vertical position presses painfully against the tongue and palate, particularly if the noseband is buckled tightly. If the horse's head is strongly flexed at the poll, the middle piece again rests flat on the tongue, and this point of pressure is less severe.

③ The so-called "Dick Christian" snaffle with an effect similar to that of the Dr. Bristol. Both of these hinged snaffles are not recommendable because of the pressure they put on the palate and tongue.

④ A snaffle bit with a copper roller that has a pleasant taste. This is to encourage a horse to chew and salivate. Smooth copper rollers are preferable to ridged ones that can cause tongue chafing during active chewing.

solution for training a young horse. Because the rings are positioned approximately three-quarters of an inch further outward, the starting points for the reins are widened, allowing for clearer steering aids that lead the young horse better into turns. A soft and experienced hand is required to avoid pinching the lower jaw, as the longer arms of the bit, extending further beyond the sides of the mouth, intensify the rein aids. However, the long shanks protect and preserve the corners of the mouth very well and also prevent the bit from being pulled through the mouth. And, if the upper shank is attached to the cheekpiece by means of a keeper, the bit itself will not turn in the mouth as the reins are tightened. This is particularly important in reference to the pointy, single middle joint of the regular snaffle, which exerts a pressure point on the tongue that is increased when the reins are tightened and the bit rotates. Consequences of this bit motion can be the horse putting his tongue over the bit in order to escape the pain.

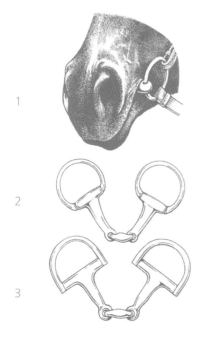

1

2

3

### Snaffle Bits

① A loose-ring snaffle without protective rubber guards for the corners of the horse's mouth. The ring holes can wear out and sharp ridges can form that painfully pinch the corners of the mouth. The snaffle should rest softly against these corners, creating only one wrinkle in the skin. It is necessary to regularly check the bit's movable parts for wear and tear. ② and ③ An eggbutt snaffle and a dee-ring, or "racing" snaffle, both double-jointed. Their construction protects the corners of the horse's mouth.

*A full-cheek snaffle with outer rings, as it is used at the Spanish Riding School in Vienna.*

A full-cheek snaffle with outer rings and an English noseband (shaded): Because the parts of the mouth are anatomically different on every horse, the full-cheek snaffle must fit well in order to benefit the horse. The stiff, leather "keeper" on the cheekpiece (indicated by the arrow) holds the bit shank at a slight angle to the line of the mouth. The following are the general advantages of the full-cheek snaffle:

1. The snaffle ring cannot be pulled into the horse's mouth.
2. The corners of the mouth are protected from pinching.
3. The shanks lie against the outer lips and provide soft steering aids, especially for young horses in training.
4. The bit cannot rotate on the tongue, therefore reducing the chances of the tongue going over the bit.
5. The full-cheek snaffle with half rings protects a horse's mouth, even in the hands of beginner riders.

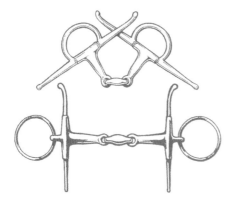

## Full-Cheek Snaffle Bits

*Above*: Variations of full-cheek snaffles: with half rings for beginner riders and with outer rings for those with experienced hand, providing the corners of the horse's mouth optimal protection.

*Below*: The steering effects of a full-cheek snaffle. If, for example, the right rein is taken up (left arrow) the left shank (right arrow) will lie softly and kindly against the left corner of the mouth, pushing the horse's head lightly to the right right during the turn. Such clear steering aids are particularly suited for training a young horse, and there are not any movable joints that can pinch the corners of the mouth.

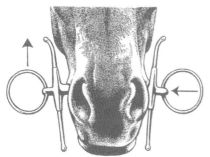

## Work on Two Longe Lines

For this work, the full-cheek snaffle is most suitable because it protects the corners of the mouth. In addition, the bit's shanks provide clear steering aids, lying softly against the horse's outer lips during turns.

Because of the gentleness of its steering aids, the full-cheek snaffle is well suited for long reining.

Long Reining Exercises
*Pressure on the horse's croup from the hands emphasizes the rein aids. With nervous horses that have a tendency to kick out, maintain a greater distance with longer reins. However, because the hands lack support at a distance, the rein aids may be less precise.*

## Summarizing Snaffles

● *Expert rein contact with a snaffle bit focuses the rein aids on the tongue and reduces the pressure on the bars.*

● *As a horse's training advances, the contact can become increasingly softer.*

● *A simple snaffle with only one joint may exert painful pressure on the tongue, bars, and palate when the reins are tightened, which lifts it into a triangular shape inside the horse's mouth.*

● *An integrated, double-jointed, full-cheek snaffle bit is the most mouth-friendly of all snaffles, as it prevents pain and is extremely useful for both rider and horse in the training process.*

# Mullen Mouth Snaffles

Unjointed bar, or *mullen mouth*, snaffles, with mouthpieces similar to curb bits that rest primarily on the horse's tongue and only minimally on the bars, are a fruitless hybrid between a curb and a snaffle. They lack the shanks and curb chain that would provide the true effect of the curb, and they lack the flexibility and steering ability of the jointed bits like the snaffle.

At best, the mullen mouth bit requires precise rein aids when a rider uses both hands. When both reins are held in just one hand, the opposite side of the bit can press against the palate, irritating the horse. Theoretically, both reins of the unjointed bar bit, as those of the curb bit, should be held by one hand in order to avoid tilting or jamming the bit inside the horse's mouth. Consequently, the mullen mouth bit is better suited for the experienced rider who already knows how to use a curb.

Since this bit rests primarily on the tongue, those made of a hard material—metal or plastic—are more appropriate for horses with thick tongues that can buffer the pressure from the reins. Mullen mouth bits made out of a soft rubber or plastic better adapt to the anatomical shape of the horse's mouth. They are more accommodating and elastic, and therefore, more suitable for two-handed rein contact. Such bits can also serve well for the correction of desensitized, "hard" horse mouths. As well, the bendable, soft rubber or plastic bar bits, in conjunction with a simple bridle without a noseband, are an effective way of preparing a horse for use of a curb bit, particularly since the horse's bars are protected.

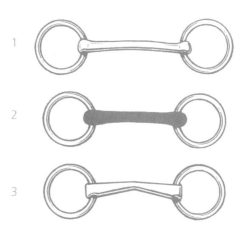

**Mullen Mouth Bits**

① A mullen mouth bit made of slightly curved metal. When only one rein is tightened, the bit tilts in the horse's mouth, so it is best suited for experienced hands and one-handed rein contact.

② A flexible mullen mouth made out of soft rubber with a metal spine (also available in hard rubber).

③ A flexible mullen mouth made out of plastic with a metal spine and intended to encourage chewing activity. The two flexible bits (2 & 3) are appropriate for sensitive or dull mouths. The rubber requires the formation of enough saliva to prevent the "eraser-like" effect the rubber can have when it chafes the sensitive membrane of the bars.

# Nosebands

A *noseband* consists of a single or double leather strap that is buckled around the lower half of the horse's head and a headpiece that positions this strap at the desired level. Nosebands combined with simple bridles enable the rider to give precise rein aids.

The simple bridle, without a noseband, consists of the crownpiece, the cheekpieces and bit, the throatlatch, the browband, and the reins. This basic leather construction does not include a jawband that encloses the upper and lower jaws, and the horse is unrestricted and able to open his mouth and chew. The addition of a noseband buckled at varying heights around the lower half of the horse's head limits the opening of his mouth, preventing an evasion of the reins and directing the pressure of the bit onto the tongue and bars. Hard or rough hands can exert considerable force on a horse whose noseband is buckled tightly. In order to allow the horse to chew comfortably, there must be enough room between the bridge of the nose and the noseband for at least two fingers to fit easily.

Since horses can only breathe through their noses, the noseband must rest a minimum of one hand's width above the upper edges of the nostrils so that breathing will not be impaired. For the same reason, you should be able to position an upright hand between the throat of the horse and the throatlatch of the bridle. Depending on its design and how tightly it is buckled, the noseband can considerably increase the severity of the aids. The tighter the noseband is buckled and the more chewing activity is restricted, the stronger the rein aids are in their effect on the horse's mouth. However, when the noseband is buckled fairly loosely and the contact is gentle and experienced, then the noseband serves to minimize the effect of the reins because the pressure is dispersed over the bit as well as the noseband. The lower the noseband is fastened on the horse's head, the more it restricts the chewing activity and breathing. The wider the noseband, the softer the pressure is on the nasal bone; thin, rounded straps tend to press into the skin and increase pressure.

The style and design of the bridle must be appropriate for the anatomical shape of the horse's head. It must not be too small anywhere, rub or chafe, and must give enough room for ear movement. Horses with small mouths, for example, are not suited for dropped nosebands because the level of the nose strap will forcefully restrict the horse's breathing.

The dropped noseband was created in order to prevent horses from opening their mouths and to refine rein aids and lend them emphasis. The effect derives from two pressure points: on the chin and the bridge of the nose. The jawband runs just under the corners of the mouth around the chin and, when the reins are tightened, it transfers some of the pressure from the bit to the chin. The nose strap must rest a hand's breadth above the upper edge of the nostrils, as high as possible on solid bone—not on the sensitive cartilage at the tip of the nasal bone—so that it does not exert pain or inhibit breathing. When the reins are tightened, the lower jaw softens and the noseband tenses. Since both points of pressure are located at nearly the same height, the pressure from the reins also transfers to the bridge of the nose,

## Types of Nosebands

*Left*: A simple bridle without a noseband is the most pleasant, force-free scenario because it allows the horse unlimited chewing activity and does not restrict him in any way.

*Middle:* An English noseband (sometimes called a "cavesson") is the mildest noseband you can use—if buckled fairly loosely. The jawband runs directly under the cheekbone around the horse's head, resting on solid, less pressure-sensitive bone. When the reins are tightened, the pressure is dispersed onto the nasal bone and the lower jaw, and it is further lessened by a wide strap. The noseband prevents the opening of the horse's mouth but still permits sufficient chewing activity. Because of its high position on the head, it does not impede the horse's breathing.

*Right:* A dropped noseband can be the most troublesome for horses because it is so often used without an understanding of its purposes and with intended force. When used by hard hands, pressure points are focused on the chin groove and the lower, sensitive area of the nasal bone. If adjusted too high, this noseband pulls the bit into the corners of the horse's mouth. If adjusted low, it restricts the horse's breathing. There should be room for two or three fingers between the noseband and bone in order to make such restriction bearable for the horse.

### Inappropriate Nosebands

*Left:* A *figure eight* noseband has crossed straps that can slip if the rosette in the middle has not been stitched tightly. The often thin, rounded straps may cut into the horse's skin.

*Right:* A *lever* noseband. Both of these noseband styles extensively restrict the chewing activity because of the straps surrounding the lower jaw, although breathing is not inhibited. The English noseband remains preferable because it only encompasses the lower jaw once and does not restrict chewing activity.

*A balanced piaffe: A full-cheek snaffle and simple bridle without a noseband, commendable yielding rein contact, free and natural head and neck carriage, vigorous chewing activity, and the horse's mouth remains closed.*

*A young horse in an early stage of training, wearing a bridle with a snaffle and an English noseband; the noseband is not overly restrictive.*

thus reducing the overall pressure effect. The nose strap runs perpendicular to the cheekpieces, and the jawband necessarily drops lower, at an angle, in order to encompass the chin under the snaffle bit.

The little rings of the dropped noseband cheekpieces, to which both chin and nose straps are attached, should be placed at least one finger's width away from the opening of the mouth and a little higher than its corners. This is so the snaffle bit and the corners of the mouth are not pulled up uncomfortably. Because horses' mouths vary greatly, you must be very careful to adjust the jawband to suit the individual.

The jawband of the noseband should allow at least two fingers between the strap and the nasal bone.

*A combination noseband with a flash: on one hand, this is a harsher variation of the English noseband; on the other, it is less severe than the dropped noseband. Breathing is not inhibited, however, the two lower jawbands limit chewing activity quite a bit.*

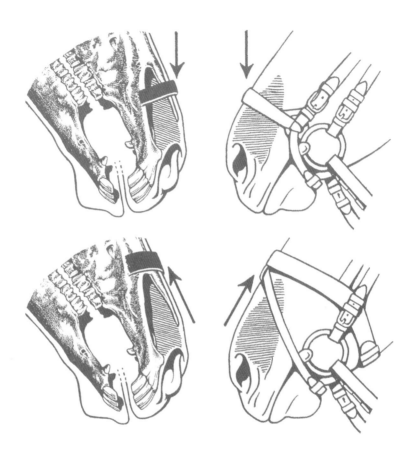

### Noseband Position

*Above:* The low position of the dropped noseband puts pressure on the sensitive, flexible end of the nasal bone and the "blow area" of the nostrils that extends with heavy breathing (hatched area).

*Below:* The jawbands of the English and flash nosebands should rest high up on the solid nasal bone where the horse is less sensitive to pressure. A wide jawband can exert little pain on this hard, inflexible skull bone and does not impede breathing, since it runs above the nostril area. Nostril and breathing areas can vary in size from horse to horse and are not related to the size of the horse's mouth. Consequently, it is important to feel with your fingers where the soft nostril area runs into the bone and where you can place the noseband so it does not cause excessive pain or restrict breathing.

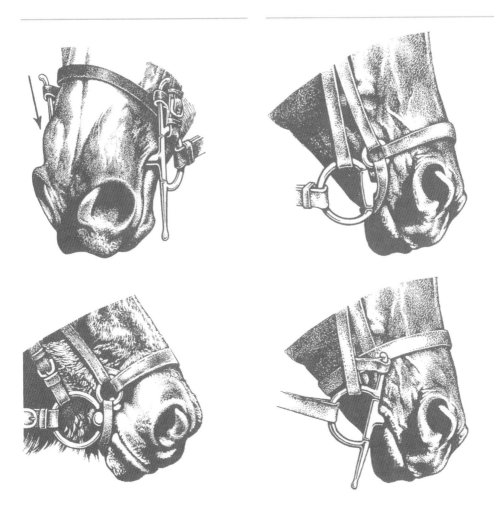

## The "Blow Area" of the Nostrils

*Above:* When a horse is breathing heavily, the "blow area" of the nostrils is easily observed. When a horse is breathing quietly, you can feel it with your fingers.

*Below left and above right:* Dropped nosebands are usually not suitable for ponies and horses with small mouths (Arabians, for example) because the jawband necessarily rests too low for them and, during periods of heavy breathing, will put too much pressure on the "blow area" of their nostrils.

*Below right:* The English noseband is the most horse-friendly style.

A snaffle bridle with a flash noseband. Because of the two straps around the lower jaw, chewing activity is quite restricted, but breathing is not inhibited.
Above: A medium canter: the rein contact is yielding and adapted to the longer frame of the horse, and the horse's neck is not restricted.
Below: An extended trot: the rein contact is yielding, and the head and neck position is natural and relaxed.

width away from the mouth openings, above the corners of the mouth, without touching the bit. The connecting straps (see arrow) keep the jawband at right angles with the cheekpieces. The jawband rests below the bit and is buckled so the corners of the mouth are not pulled up.

## The Dropped Noseband

*Above:* This dropped noseband does not fit and is, therefore, unsuitable. The cheekpieces and jawband are both too long, and the little jawband rings press on the bit. The jawband rests too low and impedes breathing. There are not connective straps from the jawband to the cheekpieces (see arrow in example below), allowing the jawband to slip down on the nostrils. The rein contact is disrupted, and the chewing activity is impeded by the pressure of the jawband rings on the bit. The overall effect is one of force and restriction.

*Below:* This noseband fits and is, therefore, suitable. The jawband rests high on the nasal bone, disturbing the breathing only a little. The jawband rings lie more than a finger's

### Rules of Thumb for Snaffle Bridles

- *Eggbutt, dee-ring, and full-cheek snaffles protect the corners of the horse's mouth from being pinched or injured.*

- *Double-jointed, integrated bits (like the KK bits) protect the palate and minimize a "jamming" effect on the lower jaw.*

- *The stronger the pressure is on the tongue, the more a horse will strive to withdraw his tongue from the source of pressure by placing it over the bit.*

- *The lower the bit rests on the bars—toward the canine or incisor teeth—the more forceful the pressure effect will be on the lower jaw.*

- *Contact with a snaffle bit requires consistent connection, a steady dialogue, between the rider's hand and the horse's mouth.*

- *Unjointed, or mullen mouth, bits are generally only suitable for more experienced riders because, when manipulated by two hands, they can slant in the horse's mouth.*

- *Nosebands should be fastened so that chewing activity is possible and must rest high enough on the nasal bone so that breathing is not restricted. There should be enough room between the jawband and the horse's head to allow two or three fingers to move.*

# Questionable Devices

"The more complicated and convoluted the instrument in leather and metal, the greater is the bungler who uses it." These words of criticism were expressed in the eighteenth century by the French riding master Francois Robichon de la Guérinière, and his like-minded colleagues, in reference to those who strove to substitute forceful aids for riding ability. Although probably addressed only indirectly, the criticism applies particularly to incorrect or faulty handling of the reins—the most common cause for the use of supplemental, coercive aids.

An old horseman's aphorism proclaims that a bridle and bit are as gentle or as forceful as the hands that are maneuvering the reins. This adage is not always truthful, as there are some bit constructions that can be highly uncomfortable for the horse no matter how carefully the rider handles the reins. Tack suppliers offer a multitude of "corrective bits" that are meant to force a horse to obey through coercion and pain. But, it is a great mistake to believe that forceful bridling with a variety of crafty gadgets—that in hard hands cause nothing but animal brutality—can make up for a lack of rider ability or correct a horse spoiled by a bad rider. Force causes tension and resistance, and tightness in the horse's head, neck, and back is the consequence.

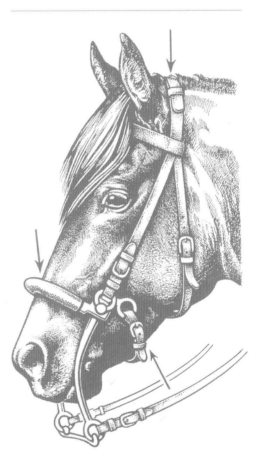

A Mechanical Hackamore without a Bit. When the reins are tightened, pressure is exerted on the upper and lower jaws and the poll (see arrows). Though the horse's mouth remains unaffected, the forceful, curb-shank pressure effect on the bridge of the nose and lower jaw represents inexcusably cruel bridling.

*A mechanical hackamore combined with a snaffle bit and connecting straps, to which the reins are attached. Imprecise rein contact and rough hands can make this a brutal and torturous tool. When the reins are tightened, the upper and lower jaws are pushed together, and simultaneously, the pressure from the snaffle affects the horse's mouth—chewing activity is impossible.*

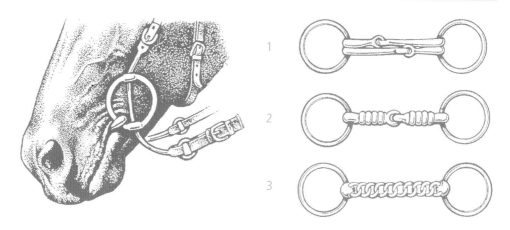

**Forms of Torturous Bridling**

*Left:* A gag bit primarily affects the corners of a horse's mouth. This mechanical tool of force is unsuitable for true horsemen. Nylon string, or the thin, round cheekpieces, of this bridle are threaded through the large, snaffle rings that have holes at the top and bottom. Below the rings, the reins are buckled into the ends of the cheekpieces. When the reins are tightened, the rings glide upward, the corners of the mouth are painfully pulled, and pressure on the poll is increased. Differentiated rein contact, like that appropriate for dressage, is not possible, and refined aids cannot be transmitted to the horse's mouth. The very slightest contact with the reins inflicts discomfort. This instrument should be strictly rejected.

*Right:* Cruel snaffle bits:

① A double-mouth jointed snaffle with irregularly long snaffle arms and asymmetrically positioned joints that squeeze the tongue, bars, and lips when the reins are taken up. This forceful bit does not permit differentiated dialogue between the rider's hands and the horse's mouth. ② and ③ A ball-roller snaffle with side-by-side rollers, and a chain snaffle, similar to a curb chain. Both of these bits have a saw-like effect on the horse's mouth when the rider pulls the horse's head to one side or another.

# Questionable Bits and Bridles

The snaffle bit is fundamentally intended for two-handed use. Its variable effectiveness makes it suitable for nearly all styles of riding and every training stage of horse and rider. It transmits the tractive force from the rider's hands directly to the horse's mouth. Because the snaffle is very flexible—having three or four total joints in the instances of simple and KK snaffles—it allows one-, two-, and alternate-handed dialogue with the horse's mouth, and can, therefore, also serve as a steering aid.

The curb bit, on the other hand, is fundamentally intended for one-handed rein contact. The unjointed bar is rigid and immovable; it must not be tilted, and its position on the tongue must not be altered much. Consequently, it is not suitable for one-sided steering aids. The play of the rider's hand with the curb is not extremely variable; its tractive force is transmitted indirectly through the lever effect of the shanks to the horse's mouth. Therefore, the curb bit is only suited for horses whose education is complete and experienced riders with sensitive hands who have mastered refined weight aids.

In order to combine the effects of the snaffle and curb and, at the same time, simplify the rein aids, hybrid bits were invented. These jointed snaffle bits with curb shanks and chains, as well as similar constructions, are highly problematic. The movable, twistable curb shanks, through greater leverage, increase, rather than decrease, the pinching effect of the jointed snaffle bit on the lower jaw. The rein aids are transmitted in an imprecise and irritating manner to the horse's mouth and often lead the rider to use rough contact. The benefit of the curb bit—precision of rein aids—is eliminated. The benefit of the snaffle bit—the ability to use refined and variable aids—is coarsened and sharpened. The advantages of using both bits together—namely, precise rein contact on one hand, and differentiated rein contact on the other—do not prevail. However, their disadvantages—uncontrolled lever and pinching effects—are increased. Even a double-jointed bit cannot reduce the pinching effect on the lower jaw.

**A Pelham Snaffle with a Jointed Mouthpiece and Curb Chain.**
In contrast to the advantages of the pelham curb with the unjointed mouthpiece, this bit has primarily negative effects on the horse's mouth. With four reins, the pinch effect on the lower jaw is increased, and if a rider uses two reins and connecting straps, his rein aids become imprecise and the horse finds it difficult to interpret them.

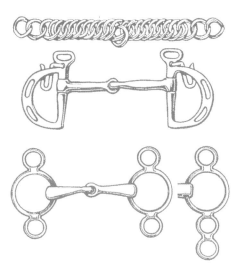

## Jointed Jumper Curbs

*Above*: A "jumper curb" (kimberwicke) with a jointed mouthpiece and curb chain. When the reins are attached to the lower part of the half rings, a light lever action will increase the pinching effect on the lower jaw. If the reins are attached in the middle of the half rings, at the height of the mouthpiece, the tractive force will be like a simple snaffle's, especially if used without a curb chain. With shanks and a curb chain, this bit is not recommendable.

*Below*: An *elevator* bit with a jointed metal mouthpiece. This bit should only be used as a snaffle, without a curb chain, and with the reins attached to the large rings. This way, the increased pinching effect from the smaller rings will be avoided.

## The Tractive Force Effect of the Pelham Snaffle

*Above*: When only the top reins are tightened, the same pinching effect on the lower jaw takes place as with a simple snaffle. The curb chain remains loose, and there is no lever effect.

*Below*: When the bottom reins are tightened, the lever effect of the curb goes into action, the curb chain is tensed, and the lower jaw is pinched. The pelham bit with the jointed mouthpiece is not recommendable for the horse's mouth—or for proper rein contact.

### Rules of Thumb for Snaffle Bits with Lever Effects

● *Jointed snaffles with lever effects and curb chains cause increased pinching of the lower jaw, induce mouth pain, and prevent precise and exact rein contact. For the purpose of dressage, these bits should be strictly rejected.*

# Auxiliary Reins

Usually, when *auxiliary reins* are used by a rider while he is in the saddle, it is an admission of rider incompetence. Auxiliary reins, made of leather or various other materials, are additional to those on the basic bridle and have varying mechanical effects on the horse's mouth. They often limit the vertical and horizontal movements of the horse's head and can do so with considerable force. Fundamentally, they handicap sensitive and differentiated contact; with hard hands and tight buckling, they coarsen and intensify the rein aids. The auxiliary reins discussed here are widely used, and often, to the chagrin of the horse, widely misused, both out of ignorance and with malicious intent.

Aside from very few exceptions that should be dealt with only by seasoned professionals, riders should renounce the use of forceful auxiliary aids because in most cases, they do not know how to use them properly and will actually achieve goals more easily through educated, empathetic riding. Even experts reject auxiliary reins most of the time, since knowledge and experience does not require their use.

Compensating for rider inability by using draw reins, for example, can cause permanent damage to a horse's health because of the extreme force that affects the horse's whole body. Incorrectly used draw reins lead to tension and tightness throughout the entire body, preventing relaxation (*Losgelassenheit*) and "throughness" (*Durchlassigkeit*) in collection. Draw reins should only be used temporarily, if at all, and for very short periods of time for corrective purposes, and they should never be applied with force. Auxiliary reins that are connected to the mouth will jerk the tongue and bars when a horse throws his head in the air. Auxiliary reins connected to the noseband affect the less sensitive nasal bone.

The *running martingale*, sometimes called "jumping reins," is an English invention that is intended to prevent a horse from throwing his head up in the air when hunting and, specifically, jumping. The mostly senseless use of this auxiliary aid is widespread, primarily because of ignorance of its rather harmful effects.

When a horse is holding his head normally and the reins are held straightly and evenly, the running martingale should hang in loops, its length dependent on the natural head and neck carriage of the horse (be it long or short, low or high). *Under no circumstances* should the snaffle reins be pulled downward by a martingale that is adjusted too tightly, causing the same downward pull on the horse's mouth, and forcing him to bend at the poll. The consequences of this incorrect use of the martingale can be permanent desensitization and hardening of the horse's mouth, as well as tightness and tension in the neck and back musculature that will harden the horse's back. The martingale has no business whatsoever in dressage training. It is intended for use in exceptional situations during hunts—and even then, its purpose is questionable since, at best, it limits a horse's head-throwing, but certainly does not prevent it completely.

Coercive *draw reins* are thoughtlessly misused primarily to cover up rider inability, pretend collection, and push a horse into an unnatural frame. The inappropriate use of draw reins is simply inhumane. This questionable device, thought to have been

**The Running Martingale**
The looped, "forked" straps must be long enough so that when they are stretched, they come to approximately the height of a horse's eyes (when he carries his head naturally).

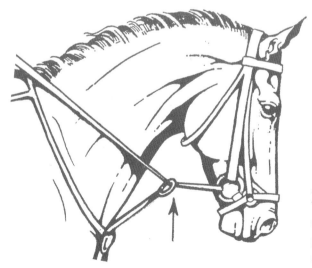

**A Martigale Buckled too Tightly.**
The snaffle reins are bent (indicated by arrow), and this painfully influences the horse's mouth, forcing flexion.

invented by the Duke of Newcastle, is either completely rejected by experienced trainers or accepted only in exceptional circumstances.

Draw reins consist of two leather straps, each about nine feet in length, that run from the girth, between the front legs, up through the snaffle rings, and into the rider's hands. Draw reins are intended to invite horses with weak, hard, or anatomically unfavorable back and neck musculature to stretch forward and downward, "without force," in order to produce the appearance of the rounded bow of collection. As a counter-force to the draw reins, the thrust from the hindquarters must be energetically encouraged by the driving aids in order to prevent the "braking" aids from being overpowering. Attaching the draw reins at the horse's sides under the saddle flaps should be avoided, as it makes the downward stretching of the horse's head and neck more difficult. If used, draw reins should only be for gradually developing and strengthening weak muscles in the back and top of the neck. They must be used with great care for limited amounts of time—only a few minutes—and should only be manipulated one hand at a time as a gentle support for the normal rein aids. As soon as the voluntary stretching forward and downward occurs, the draw reins must be released. Constant use of the draw reins is cruel and will ruin a horse permanently, causing physical and psychological toughness and resistance in the long run.

However, for longeing purposes, the draw reins can be highly recommended, as they substitute yielding elasticity for the stiff rigidity of side reins. They permit the horse to stretch his neck downward and seek the bit at his own inclination. The horse is allowed

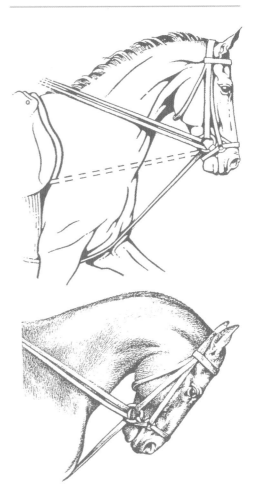

**Draw Reins**

*Above*: Draw reins, fitted correctly, running from the lower chest through the snaffle rings—inside to outside—and parallel to the snaffle rein in each hand. Attaching the draw reins under the saddle flap (as shown by dotted lines) impedes the stretching position, forcefully confines the horse, and should not be done.

*Below*: The draw reins are being misused here, as the horse's head has been seesawed down, his neck is rolled up (showing false flexion), and his mouth is experiencing pain.

**Draw Rein Misuse**

Forced flexion behind the vertical by means of draw reins disturbs the balance of horse and rider and prevents collection and upright carriage. This extremely confined neck shows false flexion, the hindquarters do not step under the body in order to carry more weight, and both the rider and horse's weight are primarily on the forehand. The horse defends himself against a too high, too late, spur stab (that only serves to drive the energy downward into the forcefully "braking" draw reins) with a swishing tail. Driving aids and "braking" aids counteract one another instead of working together, and the horse's impulsion is effectively "run into the ground."

to choose which height to carry his head and when to change that height, and through this frequent, voluntary stretching, tension in the neck and back musculature is prevented.

So, while for riding purposes, draw reins are frowned upon (and rightfully so), they serve an excellent purpose for longeing. The horse is able to determine his own head and neck position and may stretch forward at any time. When the horse is holding his head naturally, the draw reins should be adjusted so that they do not confine the neck and the horse's profile remains in front of the vertical. The longe line must be attached only to the cavesson—not to the snaffle ring—so that the horse's mouth is not disturbed and the draw reins can slide smoothly through the snaffle rings. The draw reins should run between the front legs, through the snaffle rings (from the inside to the outside), and to the saddle billets, or to approximately the same height on a longeing surcingle.

The horse is regulating his own rein contact, and therefore, a simple snaffle bridle—put over the longeing cavesson so that the bit lies softly in the horse's mouth and invites chewing—is sufficient. The horse will not feel any force in his mouth, and so at this time, a noseband is superfluous, and indeed rather harmful, because it confines the mouth. If you attach each draw rein end to the longeing surcingle at the horse's sides (as opposed to running one set of ends between the front legs, to the girth), the young horse will receive more precise guidance—an effect similar to side reins but with more freedom of movement. However, when the draw reins are buckled in this triangular form, with all four ends attached to the longeing surcingle, then downward neck stretching is limited.

When longeing, draw reins can enable the horse to determine his
own head and neck posture and independently stretch because they
are able to glide smoothly up and down through the snaffle rings.

*Correct, almost horizontal attachment of side reins. The horse's neck is not confined, and his profile remains in front of the vertical. Side reins without elastic rubber donuts will transmit a more stable connection to the horse's mouth.*

A completely force-free method of lateral gymnasticizing of the horse's neck musculature (rather than pulling the horse's head around with a bridle rein or other device, like a side rein) is feeding treats from the saddle as a reward after an exercise well done. The rider should bend downward and hold a treat (alternating left and right) close to his stirrup, allowing the horse to grasp the treat while praising him with his voice. The treat should be held as low as possible so that the horse really has to stretch his head and neck back and downward, while simultaneously arching his back upward. If you hold the treat too high, the horse's neck will stretch upward, the spine will hollow, and the desired extreme bending of the horse's neck to one side will not take place. Should the horse begin to stop on his own accord and beg for treats while being worked, you must drive him forward energetically. The rider decides the time for treats!

*Side reins* do have some purpose: when working a horse in hand, as a form of restriction when longeing, and when giving beginner instruction on schooled horses. However, they do enact a certain amount of force that can tighten the neck and poll musculature. Side reins can also cause a seesawing effect in the horse's mouth during longeing—in time with the alternating footfalls of the front legs—that may carry over to the tongue and bars.

Side reins are usually used in pairs to stabilize bending at the poll. Often, there are stretchable rubber rings, or "donuts," sewn into the middle of the straps that supply some elasticity to otherwise unyielding leather. The hook or clip on one end of each side rein is attached to the corresponding snaffle ring, while the adjustable buckle on the opposite end is attached to the saddle or longeing surcingle. Side reins can serve as substitutes for the rider's hands. In the equestrian sport of *vaulting*, for example, side reins ensure that the horse goes quietly on the bit and swings regularly through his back. During lessons for a beginner rider, the side reins keep the horse quiet and his head down. They should be attached to the girth or surcingle at such a height that they form a horizontal line to the horse's mouth when the horse's head and neck are in a natural position, and his profile is slightly in front of the vertical. Shorter side reins than this, particularly with young horses, can lead to tightness in the neck muscles.

A single side rein attached to the noseband of the bridle or cavesson has a gentler effect because it permits lateral movement of the head and affects only the nasal bone. And yet, it does limit the horse's ability to lift his head.

When longeing with two side reins, the inner one should be buckled two holes shorter than the outer one, in order to emphasize the bend of the circle. The most common error seen in longeing with side reins are those that are too short and are, therefore, seesawing while the horse is moving, dulling his mouth and tightening his neck muscles. In order to protect the horse's mouth, the longe line should never be attached to the snaffle ring but always to the cavesson. As mentioned previously, for longeing purposes, draw reins are far better than side reins because they permit voluntary head and neck carriage and stretching.

Young horses that have not been ridden yet and are just becoming familiar with longeing should be longed only with a longe line and cavesson. This way, their head and neck carriage is unrestricted, and they do not immediately feel force and confinement, which might cause them to panic. Next, they should have a chance to get used to an added snaffle bridle without side reins. Once they are comfortable with this, the side reins can be attached, but long enough so that the neck is not confined and the head remains in front of the vertical. And again, in warning, if the longe line is ever attached to the snaffle ring, the horse will feel pain in his mouth, causing resistance in him at a young age.

**The Radius of Movement of the Side Reins**
As can be seen, when using side reins, the neck cannot stretch. In most longeing situations, draw reins are preferable because they allow the horse to stretch his neck downward.

## Longeing with Side Reins

*Below left*: Driving whip aids, which should amount to a mere lifting of the whip, occur almost unnoticeably from the wrist, without any obvious movement of the arm. The horse should view the whip merely as an extension of the trainer's arm. It should be used in a humane manner—not as an instrument for beating. The trainer should turn almost on the spot, standing upright and without excess movement, in order to indicate to the horse with his authoritative appearance that he demands recognition as the "herd leader." If the horse bounds forward too enthusiastically, the trainer accepts it without punishing, gradually slowing the horse down with his voice and gentle half-halts, until the horse goes rhythmically in the desired gait.

The longe line is always attached to the cavesson—not to the bit.

*Below*: If the horse does not respond to the trainer's vocal commands, they should be immediately followed by short, precise, and sensitive half-halts from the longeing hand to the cavesson. A light, snake-like shaking of the longe line prevents the horse from coming off the track and into the middle of the circle. The horse has an innate fear of snakes, and therefore, he will instinctively move away from the lightly gyrating longe line. The lower arm and longeing hand should point in a straight line to the horse's mouth. The tip of the longeing whip should appear neutral when pointed at the air under the horse's belly but have a driving effect when it is pointed at his hind fetlocks.

# Rein Contact During the Transition Period

The *pelham* bit, without a port for the tongue—sometimes referred to as a "polo curb"—combines the direct pressure effect of the mullen mouth snaffle with the indirect lever effect of the curb bit. The bradoon and curb of the classical double bridle are molded into one bar bit that takes up less room in the horse's mouth and simplifies the handling of the reins. The pelham should be worked with two sets of reins: one set has a snaffle effect, and the other has a curb effect.

The set of reins attached to the larger, upper, bit rings transmits the rein aids directly to the horse's tongue because, just as with a normal snaffle, the reins are attached at the height of the bar. The lower pair of reins is attached to the smaller rings at the bottom of the shanks, and in combination with the chin chain, puts the lever action into effect. Both sets of reins affect the same bit. This is in contrast to the normal dressage double bridle, where the pressure alternates between the bradoon and curb.

The upper set of reins and their snaffle effect play a far larger part in the rein aids, while the curb reins have a supportive and complementary role. Because of their dominating role, the snaffle reins run underneath the little fingers, and the curb reins, with their lesser role, run between the little and ring fingers in the rider's hands. Be aware that the rigid, unjointed bar does not allow for steering aids, like the flexible, jointed snaffle. The upper pair of reins should maintain consistent contact with the horse's

*Before a horse can be equipped with a shank bit, he must receive a fundamental and detailed dressage education in a simple snaffle.*

mouth, and the lower pair should be more yielding, though not so loose as to be looped, and should never be taken up abruptly, as this immediately activates the lever effect. The curb reins produce the flexion at the poll, and the snaffle reins stabilize the height at which the horse carries his head. Altogether, the pelham bit has a less severe, but also less differentiated, effect on the horse's mouth than the curb and bradoon combination.

*In the baroque era, the horse was bridled with a curb and two pairs of reins during the transitional training phase. The rider primarily used the upper set of reins—those without a leverage effect—in order to protect the horse's mouth. Later, the pelham bit was developed from this combination. (Copper engraving: J.E. Ridinger).*

The pelham with two sets of reins provides the experienced rider with educated hands a horse-friendly and fairly precise manner of conducting the reins. The pelham is also particularly suited for the rider who is transitioning between using a simple snaffle and a double bridle, as it helps the rider learn to manipulate four reins. The pelham should be combined with an English noseband in order to limit chewing activity. Without a noseband, some horses try to play with the shank ends with their lips.

Equipping the pelham bit with connecting straps (running between the curb and snaffle rings) and then using only one set of reins is a concession to one-handed rein contact, such as that of the polo player who needs to hold a club with the other hand. Of course, when you use a pelham with a single set of reins, you end up producing rather inexact rein aids and sacrificing its advantages. The rein aids are transmitted unclearly, there is almost no lever effect, and the aids are altogether coarser and can't be finely tuned and transmitted. When attached to connecting straps, the reins cannot glide smoothly as is desired because leather connected to leather causes friction. The hands cannot determine where the reins connect to the horse's mouth: one could be stuck to the upper part of the connecting strap, while the other may have slipped to the bottom. The pressure points in the horse's mouth are uneven, confusing, and irritating, often resulting in undesired responses from the horse. Obviously, this type of bridling is completely unsuitable for dressage training!

However, when used by advanced riders who have mastered steering with their seats and thighs and are transitioning from snaffle

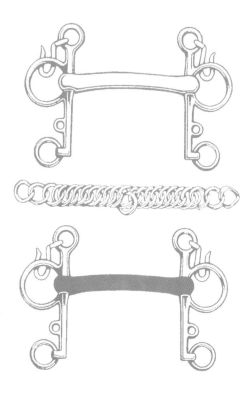

The Pelham (or "Polo") Curb with an Unjointed Mouthpiece, Movable Shanks, and a Curb Chain The movable hinges must be constantly checked for wear and ridge formation, in order to protect the corners of the mouth from pinching and injuries. Mouthpieces made of metal—or a synthetic material with a metal spine—are more pleasant for the horse. Hard or soft rubber can cause a painful, eraser-like effect in the horse's mouth if there is not enough saliva. Provided there is sufficient saliva, soft rubber bits with metal spines have proven effective as corrective bits for horses with injured or "hard" mouths.

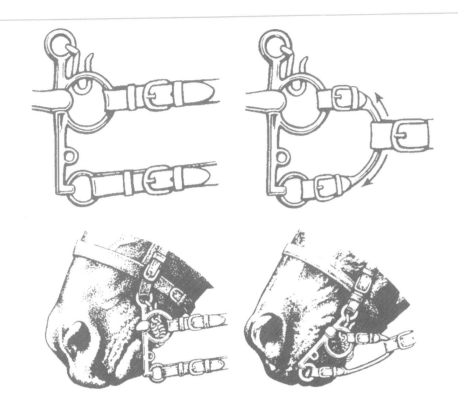

*Above*: Pelham curbs should be used with two pairs of reins—four reins total (left)—so that all the positive characteristics of balanced rein contact are felt to their full advantage. The rein pair that is buckled into the higher, larger rein rings, has a direct effect on the unjointed mouthpiece, while the reins that are buckled into the lower, smaller rings have a leverage effect. The use of just one pair of reins (right)—that is, two reins with connective straps—provides inexact rein contact. The leverage effect of the shanks is almost cancelled out, and the rider no longer has precise, finely measured aids at his disposal.

*Below*: Correct buckling of the pelham with an English noseband (left). Since a bradoon is not necessary, the points of the hooks of the curb chain point toward the horse (in contrast to those of the double bridle) and are bent outward (like those of the double bridle). This way, they cannot dig into the corners of the mouth, despite the short, upper extensions of the shanks. Connecting straps with one set of reins (right) can cause ambiguity of the rein aids, as the two different contact points of the reins exert varying pressure points in the horse's mouth. Consequently, precise, differentiated rein aids are nearly impossible.

rein contact to the double bridle, the pelham is very suitable—when it is used with two sets of reins. In the beginning, it is advisable to alternate holding the reins two-handed, "three-and-one" (three reins in the left hand, and one in the right) with one-handed (all four reins in the left hand), in order to achieve a balanced connection and refine weight aids. Later, when the rider has become sensitive to the two-sided, even rein connection, he can practice holding the reins symmetrically, "two-and-two" (two reins in each hand).

*When learning how to ride side saddle, though here a double bridle is being used, the simpler pelham with four reins can serve as a suitable introductory bit.*

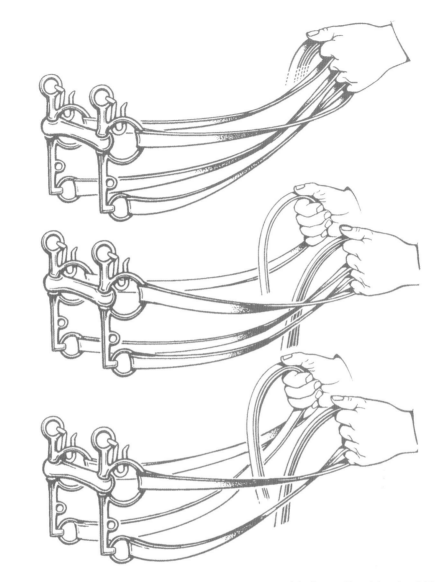

**Holding the Reins with a Pelham Bit**

① Holding the reins with one hand is good practice for achieving quiet hands and balanced contact, though it is not suitable for steering (those aids must come from the seat and thighs).

② Holding the reins "three-and-one": The right "snaffle rein" rests in the right hand, and both "curb reins" rest loosely in the left hand, in order to resist the temptation to steer with them. The rider should have a balanced two-sided connection via the "snaffle reins."

③ Holding the reins "two-and-two": One "snaffle rein" and one "curb rein" rests in each hand. This requires refined and sensitive hands for a balanced connection that does not inadvertently use the "curb reins" to steer, and consequently, tilt the bit in the horse's mouth.

# Rein Contact During the Completion Phase

In a full gallop with their heads raised and nostrils blowing, the wild forefathers of desert Arabians pounded the plains, searching for far off sources of the water that would ensure survival. The naturally high head and neck carriage of the desert horse was an evolutionary development that allowed him to smell the life-saving resource over great distances in his water-deprived environment.

When the horse was domesticated, riders were presented with the problem of mastering him. That high head and neck carriage that was well suited for scenting was not as suitable for the rider's rein contact, and a bridle that would lower the head and provide a starting point for the rein aids was required. According to legend, desert Bedouins invented the curb bit with long shanks, in order to lower the horse's head and effectively maneuver him in battles. Whether this legend is true, as according to historical research, is a matter for discussion, but it does sound logical. In Central Asia, the domesticated pony type (a descendant from the Prezewalski horse with a low-set, horizontal neck and low head carriage) was prevalent, and the curb bridle would have been senseless. A snaffle bit without shanks served their purpose.

After a thorough dressage education, the rider has internalized the idea that the horse's back and hindquarters—the parts of the horse that are largely responsible for carrying the extra, nature-unintended, weight of the rider—must be constantly gymnasticized and strengthened. This must be done, both in hand and under the rider, through diligent driving aids in various exercises. The rider has also learned that the rein aids are to be used

secondarily in order to "catch" and regulate the primary driving body aids and accompany and support them. Otherwise, the rein aids lose their purpose.

In addition, the rider knows that empathetic and sensitive rein contact can only occur if he is balanced at the center of gravity in the saddle and does not support his seat with the reins. Otherwise, he will disrupt the horse's mouth, forcing the horse behind the vertical, shortening and tightening his neck, and robbing him of the balancing rod needed to find his common balance. These rider prerequisites hold true for all riding disciplines because they are necessary if the horse is to carry the rider's weight for any length of time without damage to his health.

Those riders who want to use a double bridle and two pairs of reins must master advanced rider skills. Rein contact using both curb and bradoon bits requires an experienced rider with sensitive hands and a horse in a very advanced training stage. Only a horse that has been prepared with a snaffle, has made substantial progress with collected exercises, is gymnasticized in lateral movements and longitudinal bending on both sides, has overcome natural crookedness, and reacts to weight aids and turns without rein aids, can be considered ready for the double bridle.

The curb bit without the bradoon—like some use, for example, with Andalusians or in Western riding—is a rigid, shanked tool intended for going straight forward and one-handed, even rein contact with both sides of the horse's mouth. This also applies to the dressage curb bit. When the curb reins are held in two hands, the danger exists that uneven rein contact can cause the bit to tilt

*The levade is the most obvious expression, and the most distinct embodiment, of seat-independent rein contact.*

117

*Searching for Balance at the Center of Gravity*
Left: *In the piaffe, form-giving aids are used without rein connection, and the hindquarters are asked to carry an increased amount of weight.*
Right: *As a result of the corrective aids, the head and neck are raised, the croup lowers, the horse maintains self-carriage without rein contact and finds, with the help of the freely carried head and neck, a common balance.*

and irritate the horse's mouth. The shank effect of the curb cannot correct a rider's application of aids, nor can it correct an incorrectly ridden horse.

The curb is ineffective as a training tool or corrective bit because it is largely immovable, and, therefore, does not permit precise or one-sided rein aids. The use of the curb also does not directly affect engagement of the hindquarters or rounding of the back musculature—unless the rider's driving aids increase the thrust of the hindquarters and constitute the larger force.

## Dressage Double Bridle

The classical dressage double bridle consists of the curb bit with a curb chain, cheek- and crownpieces (with or without a throatlatch), browband, bradoon hanger and headpiece, English noseband, and two pairs of reins: one for the curb and one for the bradoon. The noseband restricts the opening of the horse's mouth. The curb bit is the focal point with shanks consisting of short upper arms and longer lower arms. The upper arms end in outwardly bent rings (the "eyes" of the curb) where the cheekpieces are buckled and the hooks for the curb chain are attached. The lower arms end with movable rings for the reins. When the reins are tightened, the curb chain limits the turning of the mouthpiece and, simultaneously, the angle of the *shanks* (the lower arms). The height of the port in the middle of the mouthpiece (which limits tongue freedom), the compared ratio of the lengths of the upper and lower arms, the length of the curb chain, and, of course, the sensitivity of the hands using the reins, have a tremendous impact on the severity of the curb.

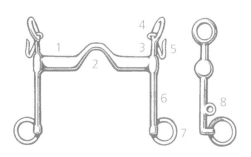

**The Double Bridle**

*The curb*: ① Crownpiece; ② cheekpieces; ③ throatlatch; ④ browband; ⑤ curb bit and curb chain; ⑥ curb reins.

*The bradoon*: ⑦ Bradoon headpiece (runs through the loops of the browband under the crownpiece); ⑧ bradoon bit; ⑨ bradoon reins.

*English noseband (shaded)*: ⑩ Jawband; ⑪ headpiece (runs through the loops of the browband under the crownpiece and the bradoon headpiece).

The arrows indicate the bridle's pressure points when the reins are tightened.

---

The Spanish-baroque double bridle foregoes superfluous leather parts that can cause sores and chafing. The throatlatch is omitted because it does not really serve a purpose if it is correctly—that is, loosely—fitted so it doesn't restrict the horse's throat or breathing. The English noseband is replaced by a nose and lower jaw strap that is threaded through the cheekpieces, and the crownpiece of the noseband can then be omitted as well.

When the reins are tightened, the noseband tenses and allows only limited

**Individual Parts of the Curb Bit**

① Mouthpiece; ② port; ③ upper arm; ④ "eye" of the curb (where each cheekpiece is buckled); ⑤ curb chain hooks; ⑥ lower arm; ⑦ rein rings; ⑧ lip strap hole.

Measured at the outer-most ends, the diameter of the mouthpiece should be between half and three-quarters of an inch.

---

opening of the horse's mouth. The curb shanks are now slanted, and the cheekpieces are tightened, exerting pressure on the poll. The mouthpiece turns a little, the lower shanks pull back, and the tongue and lower jaw are compressed between the bit and the curb chain. The horse's head "gives" in response to the compounding pressure points on the nasal bone, lower jaw, poll, tongue, bars, and chin by approaching the vertical. If the mouthpiece has a high, narrow port, the pressure on the palate and edges of the tongue will be more severe because the noseband restricts the movement of the upper jaw.

The port in the curb mouthpiece—which translates in German to literally "freedom for the tongue"—refers to the curve in the middle of the bar. "Freedom for the tongue" suggests that it allows space for the tongue to move and relax; however, the case is quite the opposite. In rough and forceful hands, the port can cause much pain as it coerces the horse's head to lower. The higher and more narrow the port, the more severe the effect of the rein pressure is on the palate and the edges of the tongue. In addition to the lever effect, the tongue is compressed into the narrow curve of the port and its edges are squeezed against the lower jaw. The pressure can be even more painful if the horse's palate is particularly flat. A thin mouthpiece can further increase the severity of these pressures.

On the other hand, a thick mouthpiece, without a port or with a low, wide port, can be quite pleasant for the horse's palate. This kind of curb protects the palate and works primarily through pressure on the elastic cushion of the tongue. The pressure is relatively mild because the bit's large contact area distributes the pressure in such a way that even the bars are not overburdened, provided the rein contact is capable and sensitive. Curved mouthpieces without ports and bits with ports that do not extend substantially above the upper line of the bar, allowing the tongue to lie relatively flat, are the friendliest for the horse's mouth.

The curb rests on the upper half of the tooth-free space between the canine teeth and the front molar teeth; above the curb, the bradoon also has to find room. Horses with small mouth openings may find the corners of their mouths are forcefully pulled upward. If you adjust the curb to sit lower in the mouth, its flexing effect will be more severe, and the horse will be able to get his tongue

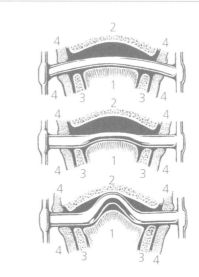

**The Effect of the Port on the Horse's Mouth**
① Tongue; ② palate; ③ bars; ④ lips.
*Above*: A slightly curved mouthpiece without a port, when used with loose reins, rests primarily on the tongue; when the reins are tightened, it puts pressure on the tongue and bars and has a relatively mild effect.
*Middle*: A straight mouthpiece with a low, broad curvature that encompasses the width of tongue will rest evenly on the tongue and bars. With a thicker mouthpiece, this bit is the mildest and most mouth-friendly.
*Below*: A straight mouthpiece with a high and narrow port; when the reins are tightened, it exerts a strong, focused pressure on the palate, the edges of the tongue are squeezed, and the middle of the tongue is compressed into the narrow port. There is strong pressure on the bars and an overall severe effect. The higher and more narrow the port, the more severe the bit can be.

over the bit. If the mouthpiece rests very high, it effectively raises the head and neck carriage, but it may cause the horse to lean on the bit. In addition, the corners of the mouth will be pulled up too high, and the bradoon will touch the molars. The curb and the bradoon have to be wide enough that, between the corners of the mouth and the curb shanks—as well as the snaffle ring on each side—there is about a third of an inch of play room so that the horse's lips are not chafed.

# The Lever Effect of Curb Shanks

The manner in which the curb shanks are attached to the mouthpiece varies. Immovable shanks are friendlier because they cannot injure the corners of the mouth. Movable shanks can wear out and form sharp, hurtful ridges; however, they do allow the horse's tongue to play with the mouthpiece and practiced hands to communicate finely tuned aids. The so-called "sliding cheek" curbs, with shanks that move up-and-down where they attach to the mouthpiece, have the same effect. These types of bits should be reserved for very sensitive hands.

The length of the curb shanks' upper and lower arms need to have a specific ratio to one another in order to achieve a balanced lever effect. When the reins are tightened, the longer the lower arms, the longer the path to the effect of the curb chain. The tractive force on the horse's mouth increases gradually and softly; however, the lever effect is quite substantial.

For short lower arms, this path is shorter, the tractive force increases in a more abrupt manner, and applying finely measured rein aids becomes more difficult. Balanced leverage diminishes when the upper arms are too long in relation to the lower arms. *Straight* curb shanks convey the force from the rider's hand more directly; *S-shaped* and *curved* curb shanks convey it in a softer manner. In competitive dressage, the straight curb shanks are prevalent, whereas in classical-baroque dressage, the S-curbs are generally preferred. In addition, a variety of curb forms can be found among Western and recreational riders.

The minimum length of the upper arms of the curb should be about an inch so the hooks for the curb chain do not rest too closely to the corners of the horse's mouth. The tightened chain counters the tractive force of the reins, initiating the lever effect on the lower jaw, while the increasingly taut cheekpieces elastically slow the lever path of the shanks. At rest, with looped reins, the curb chain should lie below the height of the bradoon, smoothly and loosely in the chin groove so that at least two fingers can fit between the chin and the chain. When the reins are tightened to the point that the curb chain is taut, the lower arms of the curb should not exceed an angle of 45 degrees to the mouth opening.

If the curb chain is too tight, the lower arms of the curb will be too rigid, even pointing forward, without much room for movement. This type of adjustment makes the curb a severe instrument of force. When the curb chain is too loose, and the lower arms can bend to nearly 90 degrees, then the rein aids lose precision and effectiveness, causing the rider to resort to tougher rein contact.

The upper rings of the curb, or "eyes,"

Above left: *A straight shank curb bit commonly used in dressage competition.* Below left: *The S-shank curb bit popular with recreational riders. Both models have solidly welded joints that protect the corners of the horse's mouth.*

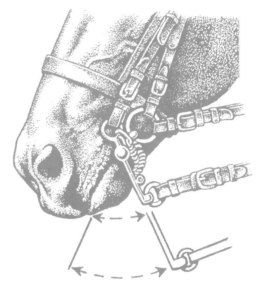

### The Curb's Lever Effect

*Above*: The longer the lower arm of the shank is, the longer it takes for the curb chain to tighten after the reins are taken up. The lever effect gently and gradually transitions and can be adjusted in subtle and differentiated steps. With a short lower arm, the path that the aid has to travel is shorter, and, therefore, the lever effect is blocked by the curb chain much more quickly and abruptly, reducing the capacity for applying refined and differentiated aids.

*A curb with rotatable and vertically adjustable shank joints (above) and one with immovable shanks (below). The movable shanks allow the horse to move the mouthpiece into a comfortable position; however, if the bit becomes worn, it could pinch the corners of the mouth. The relatively long shanks cause a more severe lever effect. The solidly welded curb protects the corners of the mouth. This particular bit has the curb chain hooks attached incorrectly, with the tip and opening pointing toward the snaffle rings, thus, possibly catching in them.*

*The piaffe, displaying exemplary gymnasticized bending of the hocks and a correspondingly balanced, upright head and neck carriage with definite rein contact (the lever effect of the curb bit is somewhat tight, however).*

are bent outward so that the thin skin covering the molars does not become chafed. The ends of the curb chain hooks, as well, are bent outward so that they do not dig into the skin. The curb chain should first be attached to the right side of the horse's mouth, then, in clockwise fashion, the links should be completely straightened and, finally, hooked on the left side so that it lies absolutely flat in the chin groove. Extra chain links should be distributed evenly on the right and the left.

It can easily be imagined that the horse considers the two bits of the double bridle cumbersome and annoying objects in his mouth. Because of the sheer bulk of the double bridle, the bradoon is thinner than a normal snaffle, and the weighty curb continually presses on the tongue and the bars—even when the reins are not taken up. Severe and rough rein aids that cause the horse mouth pain are not only a physical, but also a psychological burden, resulting in bodily tensions and inspiring the horse to question the entire aid system. In order to preserve the horse's willing contribution to the work effort and prevent tensions, or even resistances, it is absolutely necessary to handle the reins in a gentle and sensitive manner.

The most mouth-friendly, double-bridle bits have proven to be a double-jointed bradoon (like the KK Conrad model) combined with a curb with a straight bar and a very broad, low curve for the tongue, or a French curb with a curved, half-moon mouthpiece—both without ports and with solidly welded, immovable shank joints. The curb chain should be made of tightly joined links so that it lies smoothly in the chin groove. The curb chain hook points must face forward so the bradoon bit rings do not get caught on them. The total lengths of the curb shanks, including both upper and lower arms, can vary, but FEI standards stipulate that the lower arms cannot exceed ten centimeters (about

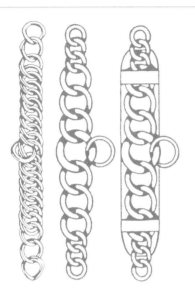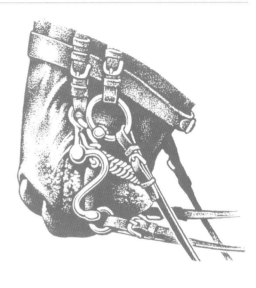

### Typical Curb Chains

A curb chain with tight links can lie flatter on the skin than one with wide links. A twisted curb chain causes painful pressure on a horse's chin. When using a leather chain guard in order to reduce the pressure from the chain, make certain that the leather edges are rounded so the sensitive skin of the chin will not be chafed. The leather will require intensive care, due to the horse's saliva. Rubber chain guards are unsuitable due to their "eraser effect." When the curb chain is hooked, the lip strap ring (in the middle of the chain) should hang straight down. On a curb with straight shanks, the lip strap runs from the little loops in the lower arms through this ring on the curb chain, preventing the horse's lips from pulling the lower arms into his mouth. The curb chain should lie loosely in the chin groove at the height of the mouthpiece, and two fingers should fit comfortably between the chin and chain.

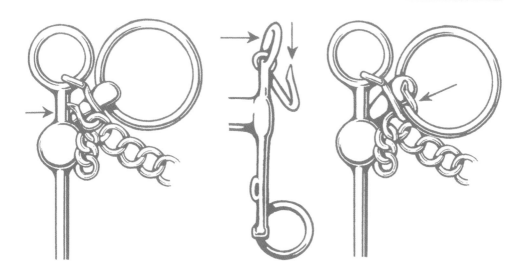

### Curb Chain Hooks

*Above left:* The tips of the hooks should point toward the horse's nose so that the snaffle rings do not get caught in them.

Above middle: The tips should be bent outward so they do not dig into the horse's skin and the chain can be hooked easily. The upper arms of the curb bit should also bend outward and be at least an inch and a quarter long so the hooks do not catch in the corners of the mouth.

*Above right:* When the tips of the hooks point backward, the snaffle rings can catch in them (see arrow). When the snaffle reins are tightened, the curb will be jammed, irritating the horse's mouth.

### Dressage Saddles

The dressage saddle (left) with a short, deep seat area transmits focused pressure onto the horse's back. The all-purpose saddle (right) offers a similar effect.

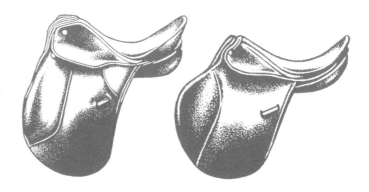

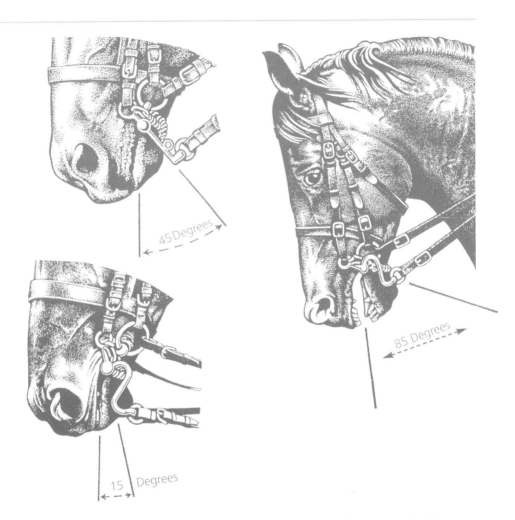

## Curb Bit Angles

*Above left:* The curb chain is adjusted correctly when the curb shanks can be pulled to an angle 45 degrees to the mouth opening.

*Below left*: When the curb chain is hooked too tightly, the shank can only move back minimally. The result is rather severe rein contact; the tongue and lower jaw are pinched tightly and painfully when the reins are taken up, and the short path of the lever effect prevents finely measured aids.

Above right: When the curb chain is hooked too loosely and the reins are taken up, the lower arm of the shank nears the horizontal. In this case, the shank has too much leeway, leading to severe rein aids. The corners of the mouth are pulled up too high, and once again, finely measured aids become impossible.

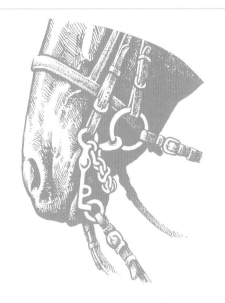

### Incorrect Curb Bridling

Here, the snaffle bit is too wide, extending too far beyond the corners of the mouth and causing a severe pinching effect. The ring hole is worn, forming a sharp ridge that can pinch the lips. The curb chain hook is attached incorrectly: the tip and opening pointing toward the snaffle ring, which it can catch on, jamming the curb. The curb chain was not untwisted in a clockwise fashion, and therefore, does not rest flat in the chin groove. When the reins are taken up, painful pressure points will form in the chin groove and influence the rein contact.

*In the extended trot, the rein contact adjusts to the horse's broadened frame. Soft contact with the snaffle reins, loose curb reins, correct hand position, and a right-angled, deep seat on the horse are all displayed. When the hands allow the head and neck enough leeway, the horse has an easier time finding his balance under the rider's weight. A free, relaxed neck, and "relative" head and neck carriage are demonstrated. The rider's seat and rein contact are commendable.*

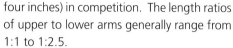

1

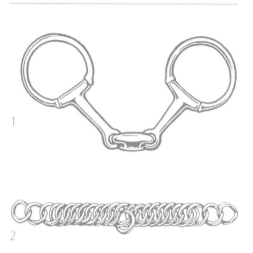

2

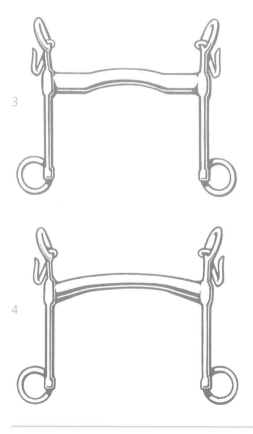

3

4

four inches) in competition. The length ratios of upper to lower arms generally range from 1:1 to 1:2.5.

Contrary to the direct tractive force of the snaffle bit, the principle of the bridle with a curb bit relies on the indirect transmission of energy—the force of the hands on the horse's mouth is transferred via the mechanical lever effect. The rigid mouth bar of the curb does not permit one-sided steering aids; consequently, all one-sided rein aids must be transmitted through the bradoon, which also permits very finely measured signals.

"Mouth-friendly" Parts of a Dressage Double Bridle ① A bradoon snaffle with eggbutt rings and integrated double joint that protects the tongue, bars, and corners of the mouth. ② A curb chain with tightly woven links that can lie nearly flat in the chin groove. ③ A curb bit with solid, immovable shanks, a thick mouthpiece, and a broad, flat port that does not affect the palate. The corners of the mouth are not pinched, and the thick mouthpiece provides a broad area of contact on the sensitive bars. ④ A half moon (or French) curb can be mouth-friendly, as well. The mouthpiece is somewhat thin and, therefore, a little more severe. It rests alternately on the tongue and the bars.

*Rein contact with the double bridle. The snaffle reins assume the far greater part of the rein aids. The curb reins only become active when necessary. The lower arm shows the correct angle from the mouth opening of 45 degrees.*

*When the rider's hands allow the horse enough room to vary his head and neck carriage, the horse finds it easier to find his balance under the rider.*

# Holding the Reins

In dressage, the rigid curb that permits only a limited range of aids is combined with the far more flexible snaffle (the bradoon) in the double bridle, expanding the possibilities of varied rein contact. The bradoon bit assumes the lion's share of the aids. In a fascinating game of question and answer, the bradoon encourages the tongue to chew quietly and the head and neck to rise. In addition, the bradoon allows the rider to steer. The curb, on the other hand, asks for flexion at the poll; this flexion must not be at all stiff, nor should the horse's face be behind the vertical, ensuring the horse the freedom to find a shared balance with his rider. It is crucial that the horse's neck, even within collection and despite the poll's flexion, remains relaxed in its full length, elastic, and unrestricted. In fact, the flexion must be so loose and yielding that the horse can snap at a fly without losing his head carriage. As a rule of thumb, the curb reins should hang slightly looped and only be tightened for a quick reprimand, and the snaffle reins remain in continuous contact, conducting a pleasant dialogue with the horse's mouth. Only in the piaffe—when the extreme bending of the hocks rounds the horse's body into the shape of a compressed spring—may the curb contact provide support for the horse. Even then, the support must not be too substantial because the neck must remain unrestricted and the horse must "carry himself."

An independent seat is a foundational prerequisite for the rider who wants to use the double bridle. To hold and handle four reins that must be shortened or lengthened at the same time, maneuvered completely

**Balance and Center of Gravity**
In the levade, the rider sits balanced, right at the center of gravity—exactly over the hind hooves so the horse can balance himself under the weight of the rider. An imaginary perpendicular line runs right through the rider and the hind hooves. In the correctly balanced levade, without forceful rein contact, it is perfectly clear that the horse "carries himself."

independently of one another, or even just held at the same length, requires much practice and agility. Supple and responsive rein-holding allows for simple, quick, and smooth transitioning between the aids. There are five styles—both single- and double-

Above, left to right: *Raising into the levade without false "lifting" reins—in fact, the reins are yielding. Only the rider's weight aids invite the horse to find a shared center of gravity on his hind legs. The levade is the exercise that most clearly betrays whether horse and rider have found their common balance.*

handed—of holding the reins that the rider can change between, depending on an exercise or his ability. All styles are founded on one where the left hand is the main component.

● To begin, take all of the reins together in the right hand. The curb reins should lie between the snaffle reins.

● Next, the left hand—its fingers spread like a little fan—comes from above and picks up the individual reins in the following order: the left snaffle rein lies underneath (and outside) the little finger, the left curb rein lies between the little and ring fingers, the right curb rein lies between the ring and middle fingers, and the right snaffle rein rests between the middle and index fingers.

● The ends of all four reins fall forward together, leaving the closed fist between the index finger and the thumb that encloses them like a roof.

● Once this is accomplished, the left hand, holding its four reins, moves from a horizontal position into an upright (or vertical) position; the reins now run, one on top of the other, with even contact to the horse's mouth. From this basic position, and with the help of the right hand, there are several possible styles of holding the reins.

When holding the reins in the second style, the right hand takes the right snaffle rein and the right curb rein so that each hand is holding two reins. This division of rein pairs requires the rider to have a distinct sense for keeping the curb reins even so the curb does not tilt or jam in the horse's mouth. Holding

the curb reins with two hands contradicts the principle behind the single-handed rein contact of the curb bit. The danger exists that the curb can become wedged in the horse's mouth and lead to head tilting or neck tightness. The rider must always return to holding the reins single-handedly, in order to prevent habitual mistakes.

### Taking Up the Double Bridle Rein Pairs

① The horizontal hand takes up the reins as they come from the horse's mouth: the snaffle reins lie to the outside; the curb reins to the inside. ② and ③ All reins leave the hand between the index finger and the thumb. ④ Fundamental style: All of the reins run into the upright left hand. This presents the starting position from which the right hand can take up two of the reins. In the meantime, the single-handed style is demonstrated in higher level dressage exercises and requires both an educated rider and horse.

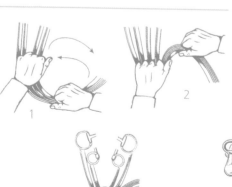

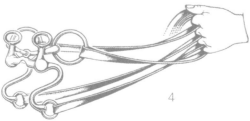

*Holding the reins "three-and-one": The right snaffle rein is held in the right hand and leads the horse to the right into the turn after the left rein has yielded.*

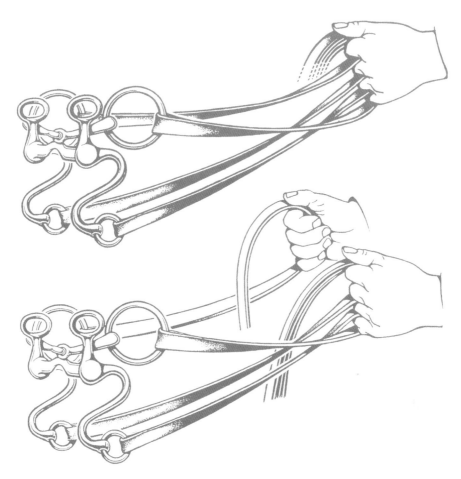

### The Starting Position and Holding the Reins "Three-and-one"

From the basic position holding all four reins in the left upright fist, the right hand can take over the right snaffle rein. In this new "three-and-one" position, both curb reins remain together in the left hand. All the aids to the curb occur with balanced pressure through both reins so it cannot become wedged in the horse's mouth. The right snaffle rein can be held by the right hand so it runs underneath the little finger or between the little and the ring fingers. The little fingers of the left and right hands can "play" with the snaffle bit, sending messages to the horse's mouth. Both the basic position holding all four reins in the left hand, and this position of "three-and-one," permit one-sided aids without compromising, or involving, the curb bit.

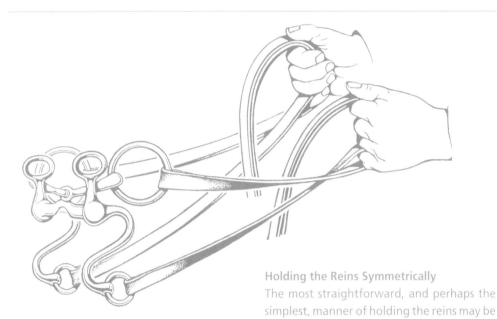

Riding with the curb alone is a traditional way of holding the reins for the high school of dressage. All four reins run through the upright left hand as previously described. However, now the curb reins are taut while the bradoon reins hang loosely. In this style, only the curb is active, providing the horse support. In his right hand, the rider, in a grand show of baroque times, holds his whip in an upright position. This one-handed style, reserved for only the most difficult exercises of the high school of dressage, requires an experienced rider with vast sensitivity in his aids, in order to maintain the utmost in collection.

*Symmetrical division of the reins ("two-and-two") with two-sided rein contact. The ends of the reins hang down on the right side between the horse's neck and the right reins.*

*Riding on the curb alone is the ultimate in rein contact for the educated horse and rider, here shown in the piaffe. The curb reins are in contact with the horse's mouth, while the snaffle reins hang completely looped and quiet. If the snaffle reins swing back-and-forth in the trot, it is a sign that horse and rider are not in complete balance. The horse must be confident in his own carriage, and the rider must have mastered empathetic rein contact to be able to ride on the curb alone.*

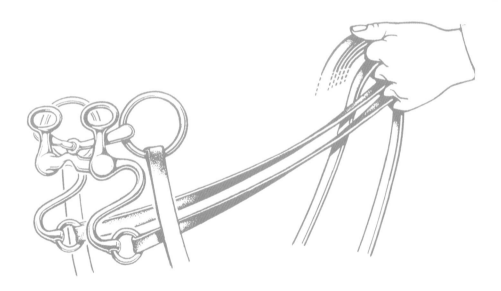

## Riding on the Curb Alone

Both curb reins are held by the left hand and remain in contact with the horse's mouth; the snaffle reins merely hang and are not used. This method of holding the reins requires that the horse is absolutely "through," has found his balance under the rider, and is "carrying himself." This method presupposes that the horse has achieved the pinnacle of training, and the rider is talented with absolutely soft rein hands. Riding on the curb alone is done merely for short periods of time and only for the most difficult exercises.

*The Fillis method of holding the reins is suitable for practiced, sensitive hands. The rider must have a good feel for balanced, two-sided contact.*

Another method of holding the reins that can have some advantages is attributed to James Fillis (1834-1913), a controversial English riding master. This particular method does not start with the basic left-handed style. Rather, both pairs of reins are held in both hands from the start. The left snaffle rein runs on top of the fist, between the thumb and the index finger, into the left hand, coming out below the little finger, while the left curb rein runs from below the little finger into the left hand and comes out above, between the thumb and the index finger. The right reins parallel this arrangement in the right hand. Fine gradations in the tilting of the rider's upright hands communicate the rein aids. When a hand tilts forward and downward, the snaffle rein lengthens, and simultaneously, the curb rein shortens. If a fist is lifted, the opposite effect takes place: the curb rein yields, and the snaffle rein becomes more taut. In this manner, smooth transitioning between the rein aids becomes possible.

*The pesade in hand in an advanced stage of training; the reins are held according to the Fillis style. The right set of reins runs in front of the withers over the mane, and both sets of reins are held in the same manner.*

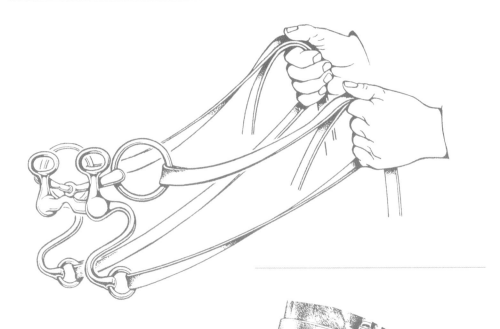

### Holding the Reins According to Fillis

The rough inner sides of the snaffle reins should face downward, and the rough sides of the curb reins should face upward, before they run into the hands, providing the best grip possible. When the hands are lifted slightly, the snaffle reins become more taut, encouraging chewing and the horse's head and neck to rise. When the hands tilt forward and slightly downward, the curb reins become active, inviting the horse to flex at the poll. This method permits finely differentiated rein aids but requires practiced, sensitive hands.

### Holding the Reins In Hand without a Cavesson

The snaffle rein runs between the thumb and index finger, from the top down; the curb rein runs from underneath the little finger to the top of the hand. This is used in advanced stages of training.

- The fundamental prerequisites for the double bridle are practiced and sensitive hands of an advanced rider, and a horse that has been properly prepared for the double bridle.

- The bradoon takes on the lion's share of the rein aids. Through it, the hands achieve contact, a dialogue with the horse's mouth, chewing activity, and finely differentiated aids. Consequently, these reins must be held a little shorter than the curb reins.

- The lever effect of the curb bit is secondary to the bradoon. The curb is used only sporadically in order to encourage and support flexion at the poll, balance, and collection.

- Immovable, curb shanks do not wear out and will protect the corners of the horse's mouth. Movable curb shanks, on the other hand, can wear out, form sharp ridges, and pinch the corners of the mouth.

- Straight or slightly bent mouthpieces—without ports—rest primarily on the cushion of the tongue. Mouthpieces with very low, broad ports rest on the tongue and the bars.

- The higher and more narrow the port is, the more severe the pressure on the palate and tongue will be when the reins are tightened.

- The longer the lower arms of the curb are, the stronger the lever effect is, though it will also come into play smoothly and gradually.

- The symmetrical, two-handed method of holding the reins, "two-and-two" (though not actually the most appropriate method for employing the curb), requires that the hands are sensitive to the bit being completely balanced in the horse's mouth.

- The term "double bridle" denotes the combination of a bradoon, curb, and curb chain.

## Jumper Curbs

Unjointed, straight bar bits with half rings and curb chains are offered in a variety of forms. The basic form is the *kimberwicke*, a bit commonly used amongst foxhunters that

*A kimberwicke without eyelets. The reins are attached to the dee rings so that the rein buckles can move freely the full length of the rings.*

**The Lever Effect of the Jumper Curb**

A jumper curb (kimberwicke) with an unjointed mouthpiece and curb chain is usually combined with an English noseband (shown here with a dropped noseband). When the reins are attached to the lower eyelets, as in this picture, there is a gentle lever effect when the reins are tightened. An unjointed kimberwicke can be used as a gentle substitution for a regular curb, or it can be considered a mullen mouth snaffle with a soft lever effect. It is important, however, that this bit does not become wedged in the horse's mouth due to one-sided rein aids.

combines the effect of a bar bit with a little leverage. The mouthpiece is attached to the upper part of a pair of dee rings, along with a curb chain, so the longer, lower part of the dee ring, to which the reins are attached, acts like a short shank.

If the reins are not attached to a fixed point in the dee rings, then they are inexact and the strength of the leverage is variable. Some models of the kimberwicke have two eyelets in the dee rings that make a solid attachment of the reins possible. If the reins are attached in the upper eyelet, there is no lever effect. If they are attached in the lower eyelet, there is a soft lever effect. The rings are not solid, therefore, they must be continuously examined for wear and the possible formation of sharp ridges that can hurt the corners of the horse's mouth.

The kimberwicke, like the mullen mouth snaffle, is used with two reins and a balanced two-sided rein contact. The hands should be educated and sensitive, particularly when the reins are attached to the lower part of the dee rings. If the reins are not attached to a specific set of eyelets but to the dee rings directly, then upon tightening the reins, the immediate effect will be the lever effect because the reins naturally hang low in the dee rings. If the reins slide upward in the dee rings when the reins are tightened, then the leverage transitions into a mere snaffle effect. So, the pressure on the horse's mouth is at first rather severe, and then weakens. This makes the kimberwicke very suitable for cross-country riding.

The *elevator bit*, or Vienna jumping curb, is best if constructed with a plastic mouthpiece (known as a *Happy Mouth*) that can adapt to the rounding of the tongue and rest softly on the bars. When the reins are

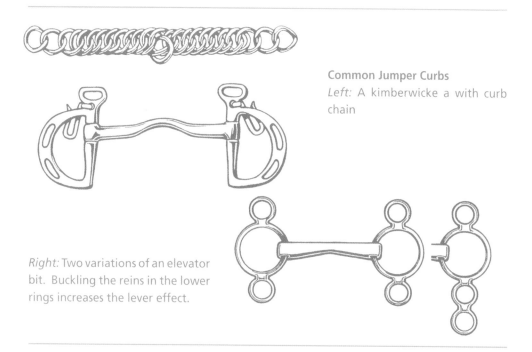

**Common Jumper Curbs**

*Left:* A kimberwicke a with curb chain

*Right:* Two variations of an elevator bit. Buckling the reins in the lower rings increases the lever effect.

attached to the large snaffle rings, it has the effect of a mullen mouth bit. When the reins are buckled to the lower, smaller rings and a chin strap, or curb chain, is attached to the small, upper rings, the bit has a lever effect. Obviously, attaching the reins to the lowest rings results in maximum leveraging. If two sets of reins are used—a total of four reins: one set for the large, snaffle rings, and the other set for the lower, "curb" rings—the rein contact will be similar to that of a pelham, only less severe.

The elevator bit must not be adjusted high and tight enough to lift up the corners of the horse's mouth. Because it is an unjointed bar, it is best suited for one-handed rein contact, however, a plastic bar—like a Happy Mouth—will be able to yield, more so than a metal bar, which, when riding with two hands, will prevent the bit from being tilted by unschooled hands.

The various options and combinations that this bit offers (use as a snaffle or curb), and a gentle, unjointed, Happy Mouth bar make this bit both mouth-friendly and suitable for the less advanced rider. That being said, the reins should never be attached to the lower, "shank" rings without using a curb chain, as the corners of the mouth will be pulled up cruelly in an effect similar to that of a gag bit.

# Traditional Bridling
## in Spain and Portugal

To this day, the conventional bridles used in Spain and Portugal are characterized by their considerable severity. This, of course, is due to the tradition of bullfighting in these countries. The work of mounted herdsmen, and bullfights on horseback, involve extensive risk. Riders put their lives on the line if they are not in complete control of their horses. At times, in order to discipline the horse and achieve absolute obedience, riders use, along with severe bridles, other instruments of force. For riders who are not in situations where their lives are in danger, these bridles and other instruments are completely inappropriate.

In the hot climates of southern Spain and Portugal, bridles consist of as little leather as possible, in order to avoid sores from horses sweating under rubbing bridles. Nosebands and throatlatches are usually eliminated; particularly the throatlatch, as when it is loosely buckled (as required), it provides little—if any—hold, and if it is fastened more tightly, it interferes with the horse's ability to flex properly. Leather fringe attached to the browband (called a *mosquero*) swings in rhythm with the horse's movement and keeps the insects out of his eyes. The regularity—or lack thereof—of the fringe's swinging

**The Spanish Curb Bridle**
This bridle is commonly used when a horse is completely trained. The reins should be held in one hand with even, balanced contact so that the mouthpiece is not tilted or wedged in the horse's mouth. Generally, the reins are lightly looped, and rein aids are indicated through a soft holding or taking of the reins, in order to reduce the severity of the bit and its lever effect.

*The Spanish riding tradition of using a curb bridle alone, here in passage. Both reins are held in the left hand so the mouthpiece does not become wedged in the horse's mouth. Consistent connection is not maintained; the reins are usually lightly looped, and rein aids are only hinted at because of the severe lever effect. It is, therefore, necessary that the rider masters an independent seat. A powerful thrust from the weight-carrying hindquarters, a forward and upward inclination of the croup, and relaxed and upright carriage of the head and neck are seen here. Altogether, excellent collection.*

movement also betrays whether the beat and the foot sequence of the gaits are correct.

Horsemen from this region prefer variations of a rusty iron curb bit that gives off a sweet-sour taste, which horses find pleasant. *Vaqueros* and bullfighters, as well as recreational riders, sometimes use the *Serreta*, a serrated iron band, as a cavesson—by itself, imbedded in leather to ease its severity, or under the noseband of the curb bridle. When the reins are tightened, the Serreta exerts painful pressure on the nasal bone, forcing the horse into immediate obedience. Obviously, this tool requires extremely sensitive hands, as this instrument can permanently scar a horse's nose. For recreational riders, the Serrata is generally unnecessary.

In the south of Spain, the trained horse is bridled almost exclusively with the curb, without an underlying bradoon. When training a horse, riders will use the curb with a cavesson, until the horse is ready to be ridden in the curb alone. In the beginning of training, the rein aids are given via the cavesson, affecting the nasal bone and not the horse's sensitive mouth. The curb merely rests quietly in the mouth so the horse becomes accustomed to its feel. As training progresses, the rider smoothly transitions the aids from the cavesson to the curb. Finally, when training is complete, the cavesson is

*A cavesson combined with a curb bridle and two pairs of reins. This is a training bridle typically seen in southern Spain and Portugal. After training is completed, the cavesson is eliminated.*

**The Transition to Riding with the Curb Alone**

*Above left*: Once a horse is fully trained with the cavesson, he progresses to the curb bit alone, which, at first, is used with two sets of reins. This is comparable to a pelham curb, as both reduce the lever effect. The upper pair of reins takes priority and has the same effect as a mullen mouth bit without shanks.

*Above right*: Trainers gradually transition the horse to the lever effect of the shanks by taking the lower pair of reins into the left hand. The *Serreta* is a detachable, jagged iron strap under the nosepiece of the cavesson (indicated by the arrows) with a severity that demands immediate and absolute obedience from the horse. It can leave permanent scarring on the nasal bone if used roughly. It is primarily used in southern Spain by Vaqueros (cattlemen on horseback) and Rejoneadores (bullfighters on horseback) who are often confronted by aggressive animals.

*Below right*: The Serreta in the form of a cavesson noseband without leather protection. Often, the Serreta is sewn into leather in order to reduce some of the severity of the edges. The Serreta requires a rider with extremely sensitive hands and is completely unnecessary for recreational riding.

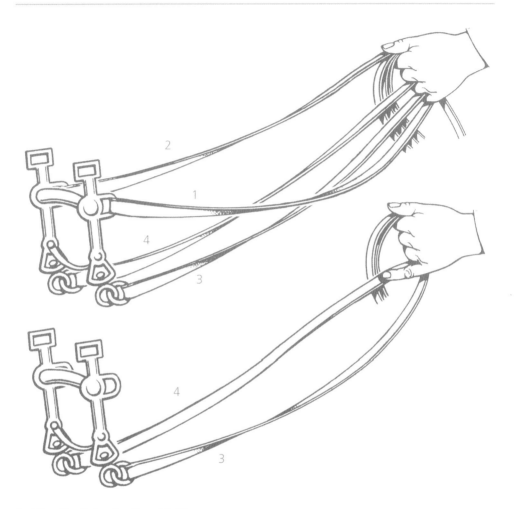

### Holding the Reins the Spanish Way

*Above:* The one-handed rein contact of Vaqueros, riding with a curb alone and two sets of reins. ① Left rein, connected to upper ring with "snaffle effect." ② Right rein, connected to upper ring with "snaffle effect," which, if necessary, can quickly and easily be accessed by the right hand for two-handed rein contact. ③ Left curb rein attached to the lower ring for a lever effect.

④ Right curb rein attached to the lower ring for a lever effect.

*Below:* One-handed rein contact with the curb alone and one set of reins (used after a horse has finished schooling). ③ Left curb rein. ④ Right curb rein. The reins are separated and distanced with the little finger so the rider can make small adjustments to the contact.

*One-handed contact with one set of reins and the curb alone while carrying a lance with the right hand. In the pirouette, the rider leads the horse around his hindquarters with solid rein connection.*

eliminated and contact is achieved through the bridle alone.

Spanish curb constructions vary in diameter of the mouthpiece, height and form of the port, and length ratio of the upper and lower arms of the shanks. The most commonly used curb consists of a slightly curved mouthpiece of moderate diameter, without a port, or with only a slight port, and with relatively long shanks. These shanks are connected to one another at the bottom with a curved bar that stabilizes them. They are immovable and solidly welded to the mouthpiece. The ratio of the length of the upper arms to the length of the lower arms of the shanks is commonly 1:3. Shorter lower arms have a more abrupt effect when the reins are taken up. Longer lower arms (ratios of 1:4 to 1:5) have a longer leverage path and take more time to act, but have a stronger lever effect, and, therefore, are altogether more severe and forceful.

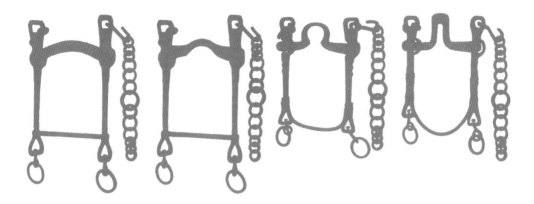

### Models of Spanish Curbs

*Above*: These bits are made of rusty iron with a pleasant taste that entices horses to chew and salivate. The shanks are usually solidly attached to the mouthpiece and further stabilized by an additional crossbar at the bottom. Some of the mouthpieces can move up and down. The two bits on the left have slightly curved mouthpieces and minimally sized ports that protect the palate; the bits on the right have higher ports, which push painfully against the palate and squeeze the sides of the tongue when the reins are tightened. On the whole, these bits are rather severe and require riders with educated, independent seats and gentle, empathetic hands.

*Below*: A Spanish Vaquero saddle with a high cantle, sheepskin, and box stirrups. This saddle provides a solid seat for the Vaquero during his work with the bulls.

*A free-handed passage with* Banderillas.
*The reins are hooked onto the rider's belt and*
*are in contact with the horse's mouth. Aids*
*are given with the seat and the thighs alone.*

On the whole, most of the riders in the southern parts of Spain and Portugal are practiced and experienced and use the rather harsh curb bridles with sensitivity and empathy; in fact, most of the time, their reins are slightly looped. The fairly free attachment of the reins to the curb shanks allows for finely differentiated rein aids that the capable rider indicates through mere hints. Admittedly, here as everywhere else, there are cases of abuse and force, where the horse's mouth is maltreated.

One example of often misunderstood and erroneous handling of the reins is in the Spanish walk, where showmanship often overshadows and, in fact, destroys its real purpose. A gross error in the contact during this exercise is a rider's attempt to "lift" the forward-moving front leg with a strong tug on the corresponding rein. The Spanish walk is not a dressage exercise in the classical sense, but rather a preparatory exercise for the stretching and loosening of the shoulders, in order to allow the front limbs to cover more height and more ground, as will be necessary for the passage. The Spanish walk also gymnasticizes the back musculature and encourages bending of the hocks. The step sequence must be that of the normal walk: after the forward and upward reaching front foot steps down, the corresponding diagonal hind foot steps down. Often, you can see that there is too long a pause between the "stepping down" of the two legs because the hind leg "drags" behind. That is, while the forward and upward reaching front leg reaches the pinnacle of its step, the corresponding diagonal hind leg remains on the ground.

The stretching of the front leg and simultaneous dragging of the hind limb result in the horse's croup stretching and his back hollowing under the rider's weight. The back musculature tenses only moderately and is not exercised to any great extent. The horse's back barely rounds and, therefore, does not strengthen to better carry the rider's weight. The dragging of the diagonal hind legs is caused by weak driving aids or a too strong, backward functioning, and confining rein connection.

Stronger driving aids will induce the horse to lift the diagonal hind leg earlier (nearly simultaneously with the corresponding front limb) and bring it further forward—it almost

**Forceful Rein Contact**

Here, the rider is lifting the horse's head and neck in order to emphasize the forward and upward reach of the front leg. The horse's spine is hollow, and the diagonal hind leg drags behind.

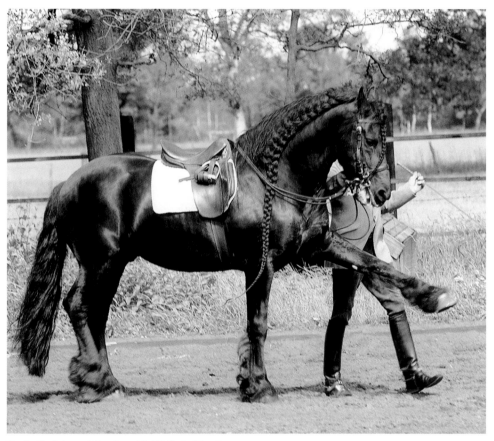

*Early Training of the Spanish Walk In Hand*
*The whip touches the fronts of the lower legs—with increasing emphasis—*
*encouraging them to stride out aggressively. The diagonal hind leg swings*
*forward in the normal walk sequence and should not drag. In this way*
*only, the gymnastic purpose of the exercise is fulfilled.*

appears to be the foot sequence of the trot. The sequence, however, remains that of the walk; the feet set down after one another, but the pauses between them setting down are shortened. This almost simultaneous forward swinging of the diagonal pairs results in increased back muscle activity and strength. Additionally, the hindquarters develop more thrust and the hocks are gymnasticized.

When the Spanish walk is done with diligent driving aids and few restricting aids, the shoulders are freed and the carrying power of the horse's back is increased. With each step of a hind leg, each side of the back musculature will alternately tense and round under the rider's weight, and the spine will "lift." Each step develops out of the horse's back. The alternating tensing and releasing of the muscles has a massage-like, gymnasticizing effect. This back activity can prevent prematurely swayed backs and provide the ability to balance the weight of the rider.

The application of the aids for the Spanish walk should be as invisible and sparing as possible. For example, when the right limb is to reach forward, the rider should give a very light, inconspicuous "call to attention" tug, while his left thigh encourages the diagonal (left) hind leg to simultaneously move forward in a diligent, flowing movement. At the same time, the left rein should remain passively connected to the mouth. The diagonal aids prevent the dragging of the hind limb and ensure that the back musculature rounds itself.

*These pictures show weaker (left) and stronger (right) driving aids that clearly depict the dragging, and then almost simultaneous reaching forward of the diagonal hind limb. Excellent yielding rein contact is shown.*

It is also very important that the horse's neck and head are not confined, as they function as the horse's "balancing rod." The horse's head must remain in front of the vertical, the rein contact must be more yielding than restricting, and admonishing half-halts should be invisible and consist of mere "hints." The idea should be to allow the horse to march on his own, the rider following the sequence of the movement, if necessary, with accompanying, but never intrusive, aids.

The optical effect of the Spanish walk—a crowd-pleasing and lovely movement—should be considered an extra bonus of a valuable gymnastic exercise. Unfortunately, the showiness of the Spanish walk often overshadows its gymnastic value, causing riders to forget about its beneficial qualities. Teaching the horse to step out with the front legs, without including simultaneous hind limb activity, degrades the whole exercise, turning it into a meaningless sham without useful purpose for the horse.

*Exemplary collection in the Spanish walk: The rein contact is yielding; the head and neck enjoy free and upright carriage; the diagonal hind limb swings forward almost simultaneously with the front leg; and the back rounds itself. An excellent presentation of freedom in the shoulder and a gymnasticized back.*

*This picture demonstrates the forward and upward reach of the front limb without corresponding activity from the diagonal hind leg. This is a sham exercise that is suitable for show only and does not at all exercise the hindquarters or the back musculature.*

# The Conversation between the Rider's Hands and the Horse's Mouth

Within the framework of a rider's complete aid system, rein aids have a secondary function. They are applied both in harmony with the rider's seat aids and independent of them. Rein aids lead the horse, indicating direction and transmitting signals that contribute to the collection process. Weight, seat, and thigh aids are the primary aids and the foundation of the whole aid system, whereas the rein aids simply complement them. They regulate the forward thrust of the hindquarters, catching the energy and directing it upward in order to round the horse in collection.

The driving seat and thigh aids always precede the rein aids, which otherwise lose their purpose of regulating and "catching" the forward and upward energy. The driver of an automobile does not step on the brake when he wants his car to move; he steps on the gas! Similarly, the rider must not prohibit the horse from going forward by holding him back, or he will destroy the desired impulsion.

Continuous, insensitive rein contact becomes an ongoing nuisance for the horse. Forceful and rough rein contact that constrains the horse's head and neck in an unnatural position behind the vertical causes mouth pain and tightness in the head and neck that, over time, can result in serious damage to the health of a horse's entire back. Consistent mishandling of the reins, therefore, is a serious offense against an animal's well-being, and must be avoided at all costs.

This book intends to clarify how to develop rein contact that is fair to the horse and allows the rider to participate in a meaningful and sensitive dialogue with the horse's mouth. It also intends to awaken the rider's awareness of problems that confront the horse as he struggles to find his balance under the additional weight of the rider. This sensitive and patient creature deserves our empathy and kindness for the many services he renders us. It is, therefore, each and every rider's individual responsibility to, at the very least, prevent the horse from suffering pain or being forcefully and inhumanely trained. After all, as the great German writer, Johann Wolfgang Goethe once wrote, "*Das hoechste Glueck dieser Erde, liegt auf den Ruecken der Pferde;*" "The ultimate happiness on this earth rests on the horse's back."

*A portrait of exemplary head and neck carriage. Even in collection, the rein contact permits the horse a little freedom to move, allowing him to use his head and neck as a "balancing rod" in his search for balance.*

# Index